POWER

POWER
A RADICAL VIEW

SECOND EDITION

STEVEN LUKES

Published in association with the
British Sociological Association

palgrave
macmillan

First published 1974
Second expanded edition published 2005 by Palgrave Macmillan
Houndmills, Basingstoke, Hampshire RG21 6XS and
175 Fifth Avenue, New York, N.Y. 10010
Companies and representatives throughout the world

PALGRAVE MACMILLAN is the global academic imprint of the Palgrave
Macmillan division of St. Martin's Press LLC and of Palgrave Macmillan Ltd.
Macmillan® is a registered trademark in the United States, United
Kingdom and other countries. Palgrave is a registered trademark in the
European Union and other countries.

ISBN–13: 978–0–333–42091–1   hardback
ISBN–10: 0–333–42091–8   hardback
ISBN–13: 978–0–333–42092–8   paperback
ISBN–10: 0–333–42092–6   paperback

This book is printed on paper suitable for recycling and made from fully managed
and sustained forest sources. Logging, pulping and manufacturing processes are
expected to conform to the environmental regulations of the country of origin.

A catalogue record for this book is available from the British Library.

A catalog record for this book is available from the Library of Congress.

Library of Congress Catalog Card Number: 2004057346.

12 11 10   9
14 13 12 11 10

Printed and bound in Great Britain by the MPG Books Group,
Bodmin and King's Lynn

To my father and Nita

CONTENTS

ACKNOWLEDGEMENTS

I am deeply grateful to the following persons for taking the trouble to comment on whatever I showed them among the arguments set out here: Vivek Chibber, Jerry (G.A.) Cohen, Stan Cohen, Suzanne Fry, David Garland, Ian Hacking, Russell Hardin, Colin Hay, Clarissa Hayward, Jennifer Heerwig, Stephen Holmes, Steven Loyal, Katha Pollitt, Adam Przeworski, John Roemer and Gail Super. I also want to thank my publisher Steven Kennedy for not taking no for an answer and for not accepting final versions as final.

INTRODUCTION

Thirty years ago I published a small book entitled *Power: A Radical View* (hereafter *PRV*). It was a contribution to an ongoing debate, mainly among American political scientists and sociologists, about an interesting question: how to think about power theoretically and how to study it empirically. But underlying that debate another question was at issue: how to characterize American politics – as dominated by a ruling elite or as exhibiting pluralist democracy – and it was clear that answering the second question required an answer to the first. My view was, and is, that we need to think about power broadly rather than narrowly – in three dimensions rather than one or two – and that we need to attend to those aspects of power that are least accessible to observation: that, indeed, power is at its most effective when least observable.

Questions of powerlessness and domination, and of the connections between them, were at the heart of the debate to which *PRV* contributed. Two books, in particular, were much discussed in the 1950s and 1960s: *The Power Elite* by C. Wright Mills (Mills 1956) and *Community Power Structure: A Study of Decision Makers* by Floyd Hunter (Hunter 1953). The first sentence of the former reads:

> The powers of ordinary men are circumscribed by the everyday worlds in which they live, yet even in these rounds of job, family and neighborhood they often seem driven by forces they can neither understand nor govern. (p. 3)

1

But all men, Mills continued, 'are not in this sense ordinary':

> As the means of information and of power are centralized, some men come to occupy positions in American society from which they can look down upon, so to speak, and by their decisions mightily affect, the everyday worlds of ordinary men and women ... they are in positions to make decisions having major consequences. Whether they do or do not make such decisions is less important than the fact that they do occupy such pivotal positions: their failure to act, their failure to make decisions, is itself an act that is often of greater consequence than the decisions they do make. For they are in command of the major hierarchies and organizations of modern society. They run the big corporations. They run the machinery of state and claim its prerogatives. They direct the military establishment. They occupy the strategic command posts of the social structure, in which are now centered the effective means of the power and the wealth and the celebrity which they enjoy. (pp. 3–4)

Mills's book was both a fiery polemic and a work of social science. Alan Wolfe, in his afterword to its republication in 2000 justly comments that 'the very passionate convictions of C. Wright Mills drove him to develop a better scientific grasp on American society than his more objective and clinical contemporaries', though his analysis can certainly be criticized for underestimating the implications for elite power and control of 'rapid technological transformations, intense global competition and ever-changing consumer tastes'. Yet he was, in Wolfe's words, 'closer to the mark' than the prevailing social scientific understanding of his era as characterized by 'pluralism' (the idea that 'the concentration of power in America ought not to be considered excessive because one group always balanced the power of others') and 'the end of ideology' (the idea that 'grand passions over ideas were exhausted' and henceforth 'we would require technical expertise to solve our problems') (see Wolfe 2000: 379, 370, 378).

Hunter's book, though much more low-key and convention-
ally professional (Mills described it as a 'workmanlike book' by
a 'straightforward investigator who does not deceive himself by
bad writing'), made claims similar to those of Mills about elite
control at local levels of US society. It is a study of 'leadership
patterns in a city of half a million population, which I choose to
call Regional City'. His findings were that the

> policy-makers have a fairly definite set of settled policies at
> their command. ... Often the demands for change in the
> older alignments are not strong or persistent, and the policy-
> makers do not deem it necessary to go to the people with each
> minor change. The pattern of manipulation becomes fixed ...
> the ordinary individual in the community is 'willing' that the
> process continues. There is a carry-over from the minor
> adjustments to the settlement of major issues. ... Obedience
> of the people to the decisions of the power command becomes
> habitual. ... The method of handling the relatively power-
> less understructure is through ... warnings, intimidations,
> threats, and in extreme cases, violence. In some cases the
> method may include isolation from all sources of support,
> including his job and therefore his income. The principle of
> 'divide and rule' is as applicable in the community as it is in
> the larger units of political patterning, and it is as effective
> ... the top leaders are in substantial agreement most of the
> time on the big issues related to the basic ideologies of the cul-
> ture. There is no threat to the basic value systems at this time
> from any of the understructure personnel. ... The individual
> in the bulk of the population of Regional City has no voice in
> policy determination. These individuals are the silent group.
> The voice of the professional understructure may have some-
> thing to say about policy, but it usually goes unheeded. The
> flow of information is downward in larger volume that it
> is upward.

So, for instance, Hunter described how 'the men of real power
controlled the expenditures for both the public and private

agencies devoted to health and welfare programs in the community', and how the various associations in the community 'from the luncheon clubs to the fraternal organizations ... are controlled by men who use their influence in devious ways, which may be lumped under the phrase "being practical", to keep down public discussion on all issues except those that have the stamp of approval of the power group' (Hunter 1953: 246–9).

These striking depictions of elite domination over powerless populations produced a reaction on the part of a group of political scientists and theorists centred on Yale University. In an article entitled 'A Critique of the Ruling Elite Model', published in the *American Political Science Review* in 1958, Robert Dahl was caustic and crisp. It was, he wrote,

> a remarkable and indeed astounding fact that neither Professor Mills nor Professor Hunter has seriously attempted to examine an array of specific cases to test his major hypothesis. Yet I suppose these two works more than any others in the social sciences of the last few years have sought to interpret complex political systems essentially as instances of a ruling elite.

Dahl's critique was straightforward. What needed to be done was clear:

The hypothesis of the existence of a ruling elite can be strictly tested only if:

1   The hypothetical ruling elite is a well-defined group;
2   There is a fair sample of cases involving key political decisions in which the preferences of the hypothetical ruling elite run counter to those of any other likely group that might be suggested;
3   In such cases, the preferences of the elite regularly prevail.
    (Dahl: 1958: 466)

This critique and proposed methodology issued in Dahl's classic study *Who Governs?* (Dahl 1961), which studied power and decision-making in the city of New Haven in the 1950s, and spawned a whole literature of community power studies. The critique was of the 'ruling elite model' and, more generally, of Marxist-inspired and related ideas of a 'ruling class'. The methodology was 'behaviorist' with a focus on decision-making. This essentially meant identifying power with its exercise (recall Mills had written that actually making decisions was less important than being in a position to do so). As opposed to what these scholars saw as Mills's and Hunter's sloppy usage, power was seen as relative to several, separate, single issues and bound to the local context of its exercise, the research question being: how much power do the relevant actors have with respect to selected key issues in this time and place, key issues being those that affect large numbers of citizens – in Dahl's case urban renewal, school desegregation and party nominations. Power was here conceived as intentional and active: indeed, it was 'measured' by studying its exercise – by ascertaining the frequency of who wins and who loses in respect of such issues, that is, who prevails in decision-making situations. Those situations are situations of conflict between interests, where interests are conceived as overt preferences, revealed in the political arena by political actors taking policy stands or by lobbying groups, and the exercise of power consists in overcoming opposition, that is, defeating contrary preferences. The substantive conclusions, or findings, of this literature are usually labelled 'pluralist': for example, it was claimed that, since different actors and different interest groups prevail in different issue-areas, there is no overall 'ruling elite' and power is distributed pluralistically. More generally, these studies were aimed at testing the robustness of American democracy at the local level, which, by revealing a plurality of different winners over diverse key issues, they claimed largely to vindicate.

Both methodological questions (how are we to define and investigate power?) and substantive conclusions (how pluralistic, or democratic, is its distribution?) were at issue here, as was the link between them (did the methodology predetermine the conclusions? did it preclude others?). These matters were explored in the debate that ensued. Critics challenged in various ways the rather complacent picture of pluralist democracy (Duncan and Lukes 1964, Walker 1966, Bachrach 1967), they doubted its descriptive accuracy (Morriss 1972, Domhoff 1978), and they criticized the 'realistic' (as opposed to 'utopian'), minimally demanding conception of 'democracy' that the pluralists had adopted, which proposed that democracy should be understood as merely a method that provides, in one of those critics' words, 'for limited, peaceful competition among members of the elite for the formal positions of leadership within the system' (Walker 1966 in Scott (ed.) 1994: vol. 3, p. 270). This conception was derived from Joseph Schumpeter's revision of 'classical' views of democracy. For Schumpeter, and his pluralist followers, democracy should now be seen as 'that institutional arrangement for arriving at political decisions in which individuals acquire the power to decide by means of a competitive struggle for the people's vote' (Schumpeter 1962[1950]: 269). The pluralists' critics – misleadingly called 'neo-elitist' – argued that this was far too unambitious, and indeed elitist, a vision of democracy, that its conception of equality of power was 'too narrowly drawn' (Bachrach 1967: 87), and that its very conception of *power* was too narrow. Power, argued Peter Bachrach and Morton Baratz, had a 'second face' unperceived by the pluralists and undetectable by their methods of inquiry. Power was not solely reflected in concrete decisions; the researcher must also consider the chance that some person or association could limit decision-making to relatively noncontroversial matters, by influencing community values and political procedures and rituals, notwithstanding that there are in the community serious but latent power conflicts.

Thus, 'to the extent that a person or group – consciously or unconsciously – creates or reinforces barriers to the public airing of policy conflicts, that person or group has power' (Bachrach and Baratz 1970: 8). And in support of this idea they cited the eloquent words of E. E. Schattschneider:

All forms of political organization have a bias in favor of the exploitation of some kinds of conflict and the suppression of

see, captures an important aspect of everyday covert and coded resistance (explored, for instance, in the work of James Scott[4]) but it is highly unlikely (contrary to what Scott suggests) ever to be the whole story. (2) is (as Przeworski's materialist interpretation of Gramsci suggests) a major part of the explanation of the persistence of capitalism, but also, one should add, of every socio-economic system. (2) and (3) together point to the importance of focusing on actors' multiple, interacting and conflicting interests. They also raise the contentious and fundamental question of materialist versus culturalist explanation: of whether, and if so when, material interests are basic to the explanation of individual behaviour and of collective outcomes, rather than, for instance, interests in 'esteem' or 'identity'. But it is (4), (5) and (6) that relate specifically to power and the modes of its exercise. As Tilly remarks, (5) emphasizes coercion and (6) scant resources. It is, however, (4) that pinpoints the so-called 'third dimension' of power – the power 'to prevent people, to whatever degree, from having grievances by shaping their perceptions, cognitions and preferences in such a way that they accept their role in the existing order of things'. It is for the recognition of this that *PRV* argues and it is this that Chapter 3 of this volume seeks to articulate further. It was and remains the present author's conviction that no view of power can be adequate unless it can offer an account of this kind of power.

PRV was a *very* small book, yet it generated a surprisingly large amount of comment, much of it critical, from a great many quarters, both academic and political. It continues to do so, and that is one reason that has persuaded me to yield to its publisher's repeated requests to republish it together with a reconsideration of its argument and, more widely, of the rather large topic it takes on. A second reason is that its mistakes and inadequacies are, I believe, rather instructive, and rendered the more so in prose that makes them clearly visible (for, as the seventeenth-century naturalist John Ray observed, 'He that uses many words for explaining any subject, doth, like the cuttle-fish, hide himself for the most part, in his own ink'). So I have decided to reproduce the original text virtually unaltered, alongside this introduction, which sets it in context.

There are two subsequent chapters. The first of these (Chapter 2) broadens the discussion by situating the reprinted text and its claims on a map of the conceptual terrain that power occupies. The chapter begins by asking whether, in the face of unending disagreements about how to define it and study it, we need the concept of power at all and, if we do, what we need it for – what role it plays in our lives. I argue that these disagreements matter because how much power you see in the social world and where you locate it depends on how you conceive of it, and these disagreements are in part moral and political, and inescapably so. But the topic of *PRV*, and much writing and thinking about power, is more specific: it concerns power *over* another or others and, more specifically still, power as domination. *PRV* focuses on this and asks: how do the powerful secure the compliance of those they dominate – and, more specifically, how do they secure their *willing* compliance? The rest of the chapter considers the ultra-radical answer offered to this question by Michel Foucault, whose massively influential writings about power have been taken to imply that there is no escaping domination, that it is 'everywhere' and there is no freedom from it or reasoning independent of it. But, I argue, there is no need to accept this ultra-radicalism, which derives from the rhetoric rather than the substance of Foucault's work – work which has generated major new insights and much valuable research into modern forms of domination.

Chapter 3 defends and elaborates *PRV*'s answer to the question, but only after indicating some of its mistakes and inadequacies. It was a mistake to define power by 'saying that *A* exercises power over *B* when *A* affects *B* in a manner contrary to *B*'s interests'. Power is a capacity not the exercise of that capacity (it may never be, and never need to be, exercised); and you can be powerful by satisfying and advancing others' interests: *PRV*'s topic, power as domination, is only one species of power. Moreover, it was inadequate in confining the discussion to binary relations between actors assumed to have unitary interests, failing to consider the ways in which everyone's interests are multiple, conflicting and of different kinds. The defence consists in making the case for the existence of power as the imposition of internal constraints. Those subject to it are led to acquire beliefs and form desires that result in their consenting or adapting to being dominated, in coercive and non-coercive settings. I consider and rebut two kinds of objection: first, James Scott's argument that such power is non-existent or extremely rare, because the dominated are always and everywhere resisting, covertly or overtly; and second, Jon Elster's idea that willing compliance to domination simply *cannot* be brought about by such power. Both John Stuart Mill's account of the subjection of Victorian women and the work of Pierre Bourdieu on the acquisition and maintenance of 'habitus' appeal to the workings of power, leading those subject to it to see their condition as 'natural' and even to value it, and to fail to recognize the sources of their desires and beliefs. These and other mechanisms constitute power's third dimension when it works against people's interests by misleading them, thereby distorting their judgment. To say that such power involves the concealment of people's 'real interests' by 'false consciousness' evokes bad historical memories and can appear both patronizing and presumptuous, but there is, I argue, nothing inherently illiberal or paternalist about these notions, which, suitably refined, remain crucial to understanding the third dimension of power.

1

POWER: A RADICAL VIEW

1 Introduction

This chapter presents a conceptual analysis of power. In it I shall argue for a view of power (that is, a way of identifying it) which is radical in both the theoretical and political senses (and I take these senses in this context to be intimately related). The view I shall defend is, I shall suggest, ineradicably evaluative and 'essentially contested' (Gallie 1955–6)[1] on the one hand; and empirically applicable on the other. I shall try to show why this view is superior to alternative views. I shall further defend its evaluative and contested character as no defect, and I shall argue that it is 'operational', that is, empirically useful in that hypotheses can be framed in terms of it that are in principle verifiable and falsifiable (despite currently canvassed arguments to the contrary). And I shall even give examples of such hypotheses – some of which I shall go so far as to claim to be true.

In the course of my argument, I shall touch on a number of issues – methodological, theoretical and political. Among the methodological issues are the limits of behaviourism, the role of values in explanation, and methodological individualism. Among the theoretical issues are questions about the limits or bias of pluralism, about false consciousness and about real interests. Among the political issues are the famous three key issue areas studied by Robert Dahl (Dahl 1961) in New Haven (urban redevelopment, public education and political nominations), poverty and race relations in Baltimore, and air pollution. These matters will not be discussed in their own right, but merely alluded to at relevant points in the argument. That argument is, of its very nature, controversial. And indeed, that it is so is an essential part of my case.

The argument starts by considering a view of power and related concepts which has deep historical roots (notably in the thought of Max Weber) and achieved great influence among American political scientists in the 1960s through the work of Dahl and his fellow pluralists. That view was criticized as superficial and restrictive, and as leading to an unjustified celebration of American pluralism, which it portrayed as meeting the requirements of democracy, notably by Peter Bachrach and Morton S. Baratz in a famous and influential article, 'The Two Faces of Power' (1962) and a second article (Bachrach and Baratz 1963), which were later incorporated (in modified form) in their book *Power and Poverty* (1970). Their argument was in turn subjected to vigorous counter-attack by the pluralists, especially Nelson Polsby (1968), Raymond Wolfinger (1971a, 1971b) and Richard Merelman (1968a, 1968b); but it has also attracted some very interesting defences, such as that by Frederick Frey (1971) and at least one extremely interesting empirical application, in Matthew Crenson's book *The Un-Politics of Air Pollution* (Crenson 1971). My argument will be that the pluralists' view was indeed inadequate for the reasons Bachrach and Baratz advance, and that their view gets further, but that it in turn does not get far enough and is in need of radical toughening. My strategy will be to sketch three conceptual maps, which will, I hope, reveal the distinguishing features of these three views of power: that is, the view of the pluralists (which I shall call the one-dimensional view); the view of their critics (which I shall call the two-dimensional view); and a third view of power (which I shall call the three-dimensional view). I shall then discuss the respective strengths and weaknesses of these three views,

15

and I shall try to show, with examples, that the third view allows one to give a deeper and more satisfactory analysis of power relations than either of the other two.

2 The One-Dimensional View

This is often called the 'pluralist' view of power, but that label is already misleading, since it is the aim of Dahl, Polsby, Wolfinger and others to demonstrate that power (as they identify it) is, in fact, distributed pluralistically in, for instance, New Haven and, more generally, in the United States' political system as a whole. To speak, as these writers do, of a 'pluralist view' of, or 'pluralist approach' to, power, or of a 'pluralist methodology', is to imply that the pluralists' conclusions are already built into their concepts, approach and method. I do not, in fact, think that this is so. I think that these are capable of generating non-pluralist conclusions in certain cases. Their view yields elitist conclusions when applied to elitist decision-making structures, and pluralist conclusions when applied to pluralist decision-making structures (and also, as I shall argue, pluralist conclusions when applied to structures which it identifies as pluralist, but other views of power do not). So, in attempting to characterize it, I shall identify its distinguishing features independently of the pluralist conclusions it has been used to reach.

In his early article 'The Concept of Power', Dahl describes his 'intuitive idea of power' as 'something like this: A has power over B to the extent that he can get B to do something that B would not otherwise do' (Dahl 1957, in Bell, Edwards and Harrison Wagner (eds) 1969: 80). A little later in the same article he describes his 'intuitive view of the power relation' slightly differently: it seemed, he writes, 'to involve a successful attempt by A to get a to do something he would not otherwise do' (ibid., p. 82). Note that the first statement refers to A's capacity ('... to the extent that he can get B to do something ...'), while the second specifies a successful attempt − this, of course, being the difference between potential and actual power, between its possession and its exercise. It is the latter – the exercise of power – which is central to this view of power (in reaction to the so-called 'elitists'' focus on power reputations). Dahl's central method in *Who Governs?* is to 'determine for each decision which participants had initiated alternatives that were finally adopted, had vetoed alternatives initiated by others, or had proposed alternatives that were turned down. These actions were then tabulated as individual "successes" or "defeats". The participants with the greatest proportion of successes out of the total number of successes were then considered to be the most influential' (Dahl 1961: 336).[2] In short, as Polsby writes, 'In the pluralist approach ... an attempt is made to study specific outcomes in order to determine who actually prevails in community decision-making' (Polsby 1963: 113). The stress here is on the study of concrete, observable *behaviour*. The researcher, according to Polsby, 'should study actual behavior, either at first hand or by reconstructing behavior from documents, informants, newspapers, and other appropriate sources' (ibid., p. 121). Thus the pluralist methodology, in Merelman's words, 'studied actual behavior, stressed operational definitions, and turned up evidence. Most important, it seemed to produce reliable conclusions which met the canons of science' (Merelman 1968a: 451).

(It should be noted that among pluralists, 'power', 'influence', etc., tend to be used interchangeably, on the assumption that there is a 'primitive notion that seems to lie behind *all* of these concepts' (Dahl 1957, in Bell, Edwards and Harrison Wagner (eds) 1969: 80). *Who Governs?* speaks mainly of 'influence', while Polsby speaks mainly of 'power'.)

The focus on observable behaviour in identifying power involves the pluralists in studying *decision-making* as their central task. Thus for Dahl power can be analysed only after 'careful examination of a series of concrete decisions' (1958: 466); and Polsby writes

one can conceive of 'power' – 'influence' and 'control' are serviceable synonyms – as the capacity of one actor to do something affecting another actor, which changes the probable pattern of specified future events. This can be envisaged most easily in a decision-making situation. (1963: 3–4)

and he argues that identifying 'who prevails in decision-making' seems 'the best way to determine which individuals and groups have "more" power in social life, because direct conflict between actors presents a situation most closely approximating an experimental test of their capacities to affect outcomes' (p. 4). As this last quotation shows, it is assumed that the 'decisions' involve 'direct', i.e. actual and observable, *conflict*. Thus Dahl maintains that one can only strictly test the hypothesis of a ruling class if there are '. . . cases involving key political decisions in which the preferences of the hypothetical ruling elite run counter to those of any other likely group that might be suggested', and '. . . in such cases, the preferences of the elite regularly prevail' (Dahl 1958: 466). The pluralists speak of the decisions being about *issues* in selected [key] 'issue-areas' – the assumption again being that such issues are controversial and involve actual conflict. As Dahl writes, it is 'a necessary though possibly not a sufficient condition that the key issue should involve actual disagreement in preferences among two or more groups' (p. 467).

So we have seen that the pluralists see their focus on behaviour in the making of decisions over key or important issues as involving actual, observable conflict. Note that this implication is not required by either Dahl's or Polsby's definition of power, which merely require that A can or does succeed in affecting what B does. And indeed in *Who Governs?* Dahl is quite sensitive to the operation of power or influence in the absence of conflict: indeed he even writes that a 'rough test of a person's overt or covert influence is the frequency with which he successfully initiates an important policy over the opposition of others, or vetoes policies initiated by others, or *initiates a policy where no opposition appears* [sic]' (Dahl 1961: 66).[3] This, however, is just one among a number of examples of how the text of *Who Governs?* is more subtle and profound than the general conceptual and methodological pronouncements of its author and his colleagues;[4] it is in contradiction with their conceptual framework and their methodology. In other words, it represents an insight which this one-dimensional view of power is unable to exploit.

Conflict, according to that view, is assumed to be crucial in providing an experimental test of power attributions: without it the exercise of power will, it seems to be thought, fail to show up. What is the conflict between? The answer is: between preferences, that are assumed to be consciously made, exhibited in actions, and thus to be discovered by observing people's behaviour. Furthermore, the pluralists assume that *interests* are to be understood as policy preferences – so that a conflict of interests is equivalent to a conflict of preferences. They are opposed to any suggestion that interests might be unarticulated or unobservable, and above all, to the idea that people might actually be mistaken about, or unaware of, their own interests. As Polsby writes

> rejecting this presumption of 'objectivity of interests', we may view instances of intraclass disagreement as intraclass conflict of interests, and interclass agreement as interclass harmony of interests. To maintain the opposite seems perverse. If information about the actual behavior of groups in the community is not considered relevant when it is different from the researcher's expectations, then it is impossible ever to disprove the empirical propositions of the stratification theory [which postulate class interests], and they will then have to be regarded as metaphysical rather than empirical statements. The presumption that the 'real' interests of a class can be assigned to them by an analyst allows the analyst to charge 'false class consciousness' when the class in question disagrees with the analyst. (Polsby 1963: 22–3)[5]

Thus I conclude that this first, one-dimensional, view of power involves a focus on *behaviour* in the making of *decisions* on *issues* over which there is an observable *conflict* of (subjective) *interests*, seen as express policy preferences, revealed by political participation.

3   The Two-Dimensional View

In their critique of this view, Bachrach and Baratz argue that it
is restrictive and, in virtue of that fact, gives a misleadingly san-
guine pluralist picture of American politics. Power, they claim,
has two faces. The first face is that already considered, according
to which 'power is totally embodied and fully reflected in "concrete decisions" or in activity bearing directly upon their
making' (1970: 7). As they write

> Of course power is exercised when A participates in the
> making of decisions that affect B. Power is also exercised
> when A devotes his energies to creating or reinforcing social
> and political values and institutional practices that limit the
> scope of the political process to public consideration of only
> those issues which are comparatively innocuous to A. To the
> extent that A succeeds in doing this, B is prevented, for all
> practical purposes, from bringing to the fore any issues that
> might in their resolution be seriously detrimental to A's set of
> preferences.   (p. 7)

Their 'central point' is this: 'to the extent that a person
or group – consciously or unconsciously – creates or reinforces
barriers to the public airing of policy conflicts, that person or
group has power' (p. 8), and they cite Schattschneider's famous
and often-quoted words:

> All forms of political organization have a bias in favour of the
> exploitation of some kinds of conflict and the suppression
> of others, because *organization is the mobilization of bias*. Some
> issues are organized into politics while others are organized
> out.   (Schattschneider 1960: 71)

The importance of Bachrach and Baratz's work is that they
bring this crucially important idea of the 'mobilization of bias'
into the discussion of power. It is, in their words,

a set of predominant values, beliefs, rituals, and institutional procedures ('rules of the game') that operate systematically and consistently to the benefit of certain persons and groups at the expense of others. Those who benefit are placed in a preferred position to defend and promote their vested interests. More often than not, the 'status quo defenders' are a minority or elite group within the population in question. Elitism, however, is neither foreordained nor omnipresent: as opponents of the war in Viet Nam can readily attest, the mobilization of bias can and frequently does benefit a clear majority. (1970: 43–4)

What, then, does this second, two-dimensional view of power amount to? What does its conceptual map look like? Answering this question poses a difficulty because Bachrach and Baratz use the term 'power' in two distinct senses. On the one hand, they use it in a general way to refer to all forms of successful control by A over B – that is, of A's securing B's compliance. Indeed, they develop a whole typology (which is of great interest) of forms of such control – forms that they see as types of power in either of its two faces. On the other hand, they label one of these types 'power' – namely, the securing of compliance through the threat of sanctions. In expounding their position, we can, however, easily eliminate this confusion by continuing to speak of the first sense as 'power', and by speaking of the second as 'coercion'.

Their typology of 'power', then, embraces coercion, influence, authority, force and manipulation. *Coercion*, as we have seen, exists where A secures B's compliance by the threat of deprivation where there is 'a conflict over values or course of action between A and B' (p. 24).[6] *Influence* exists where A, 'without resorting to either a tacit or an overt threat of severe deprivation, causes [B] to change his course of action' (p. 30). In a situation involving *authority*, 'B complies because he recognises that [A's] command is reasonable in terms of his own values' – either because its content is legitimate and reasonable or because

21

it has been arrived at through a legitimate and reasonable procedure (pp. 34, 37). In the case of *force*, *A* achieves his objectives in the face of *B*'s noncompliance by stripping him of the choice between compliance and noncompliance. And *manipulation* is, thus, an 'aspect' or sub-concept of force (and distinct from coercion, influence and authority), since here 'compliance is forthcoming in the absence of recognition on the complier's part either of the source or the exact nature of the demand upon him' (p. 28).

The central thrust of Bachrach and Baratz's critique of the pluralists' one-dimensional view of power is, up to a point, *antibehavioural*: that is, they claim that it 'unduly emphasises the importance of initiating, deciding, and vetoing' and, as a result, takes 'no account of the fact that power may be, and often is, exercised by confining the scope of decision-making to relatively "safe" issues' (p. 6). On the other hand, they do insist (at least in their book – in response to critics who maintained that if *B* fails to act because he anticipates *A*'s reaction, nothing has occurred and one has a 'non-event', incapable of empirical verification) that their so-called nondecisions which confine the scope of decision-making are themselves (observable) *decisions*. These, however, may not be overt or specific to a given issue or even consciously taken to exclude potential challengers, of whom the status quo defenders may well be unaware. Such unawareness 'does not mean, however, that the dominant group will refrain from making nondecisions that protect or promote their dominance. Simply supporting the established political process tends to have this effect' (p. 50).

A satisfactory analysis, then, of two-dimensional power involves examining both *decision-making* and *nondecision-making*. A decision is 'a choice among alternative modes of action' (p. 39); a nondecision is 'a decision that results in suppression or thwarting of a latent or manifest challenge to the values or interests of the decision-maker' (p. 44). Thus, nondecision-making is 'a means by which demands for change in the existing allocation of benefits and privileges in the community can be suffocated before they are even voiced; or kept covert; or killed before they gain access to the relevant decision-making arena; or, failing all these things, maimed or destroyed in the decision-implementing stage of the policy process' (p. 44).

In part, Bachrach and Baratz are, in effect, redefining the boundaries of what is to count as a political issue. For the pluralists those boundaries are set by the political system being observed, or rather by the elites within it: as Dahl writes, 'a political issue can hardly be said to exist unless and until it commands the attention of a significant segment of the political stratum' (Dahl 1961: 92). The observer then picks out certain of these issues as obviously important or 'key' and analyses decision-making with respect to them. For Bachrach and Baratz, by contrast, it is crucially important to identify *potential issues* which nondecision-making prevents from being actual. In their view, therefore, 'important' or 'key' issues may be actual or, most probably, potential – a key issue being 'one that involves a genuine challenge to the resources of power or authority of those who currently dominate the process by which policy outputs in the system are determined', that is, 'a demand for enduring transformation in both the manner in which values are allocated in the polity . . . and the value allocation itself' (Bachrach and Baratz 1970: 47–8).

Despite this crucial difference with the pluralists, Bachrach and Baratz's analysis has one significant feature in common with theirs: namely, the stress on actual, observable *conflict*, overt or covert. Just as the pluralists hold that power in decision-making only shows up where there is conflict, Bachrach and Baratz assume the same to be true in cases of nondecision-making. Thus they write that if 'there is no conflict, overt or covert, the presumption must be that there is consensus on the prevailing allocation of values, in which case nondecision-making is impossible' (p. 49). In the absence of such conflict, they argue, 'there is no way accurately to judge whether the thrust of a decision really is to thwart or prevent serious consideration of a demand for change that is potentially threatening to the decision-maker' (p. 50). If 'there appears to be universal acquiescence in the status quo', then it will not be possible 'to determine empirically whether the consensus is genuine or instead has been enforced through nondecision-making' – and they rather quaintly add that 'analysis of this problem is beyond the reach of a political analyst and perhaps can only be fruitfully analysed by a philosopher' (p. 49).

This last remark seems to suggest that Bachrach and Baratz are unsure whether they mean that nondecision-making power cannot be exercised in the absence of observable conflict or that we could never know if it was. However that may be, the conflict they hold to be necessary is between the *interests* of those engaged in nondecision-making and the interests of those they exclude from a hearing within the political system. How are the latter interests to be identified? Bachrach and Baratz answer thus: the observer

> must determine if those persons and groups apparently disfavored by the mobilization of bias have grievances, overt or covert ... overt grievances are those that have already been expressed and have generated an issue within the political system, whereas covert ones are still *outside* the system.

The latter have 'not been recognized as "worthy" of public attention and controversy', but they are 'observable in their aborted form to the investigator' (p. 49). In other words, Bachrach and Baratz have a wider concept of 'interests' than the pluralists – though it remains a concept of subjective rather than objective interests. Whereas the pluralist considers as interests the policy preferences exhibited by the behaviour of all citizens who are assumed to be within the political system, Bachrach and Baratz also consider the preferences exhibited by the behaviour of those who are partly or wholly excluded from the political system, in the form of overt or covert grievances. In both cases the assumption is that the interests are consciously articulated and observable.

So I conclude that the two-dimensional view of power involves a *qualified critique* of the *behavioural focus* of the first view

(I say qualified because it is still assumed that nondecision-making is a form of decision-making) and it allows for consideration of the ways in which *decisions* are prevented from being taken on *potential issues* over which there is an observable *conflict* of (subjective) *interests*, seen as embodied in express policy preferences and sub-political grievances.

4   The Three-Dimensional View

There is no doubt that the two-dimensional view of power represents a major advance over the one-dimensional view: it incorporates into the analysis of power relations the question of the control over the agenda of politics and of the ways in which potential issues are kept out of the political process. None the less, it is, in my view, inadequate on three counts.

In the first place, its critique of behaviourism is too qualified, or, to put it another way, it is still too committed to behaviourism – that is, to the study of overt, 'actual behaviour', of which 'concrete decisions' in situations of conflict are seen as paradigmatic. In trying to assimilate all cases of exclusion of potential issues from the political agenda to the paradigm of a decision, it gives a misleading picture of the ways in which individuals and, above all, groups and institutions succeed in excluding potential issues from the political process. Decisions are choices consciously and intentionally made by individuals between alternatives, whereas the bias of the system can be mobilized, recreated and reinforced in ways that are neither consciously chosen nor the intended result of particular individuals' choices. As Bachrach and Baratz themselves maintain, the domination of defenders of the status quo may be so secure and pervasive that they are unaware of any potential challengers to their position and thus of any alternatives to the existing political process, whose bias they work to maintain. As 'students of power and its consequences', they write, 'our main concern is not whether the defenders of the status quo use their power consciously, but rather if and how they exercise it and what effects it has on the political process and other actors within the system' (Bachrach and Baratz 1970: 50).

Moreover, the bias of the system is not sustained simply by a series of individually chosen acts, but also, most importantly, by the socially structured and culturally patterned behaviour of groups, and practices of institutions, which may indeed be manifested by individuals' inaction. Bachrach and Baratz follow the pluralists in adopting too methodologically individualist a view of power. In this both parties follow in the steps of Max Weber, for whom power was the probability of *individuals realizing their wills* despite the resistance of others, whereas the power to control the agenda of politics and exclude potential issues cannot be adequately analysed unless it is seen as a function of collective forces and social arrangements.[7] There are, in fact, two separable cases here. First, there is the phenomenon of collective action, where the policy or action of a collectivity (whether a group, e.g. a class, or an institution, e.g. a political party or an industrial corporation) is manifest, but not attributable to particular individuals' decisions or behaviour. Second, there is the phenomenon of 'systemic' or organizational effects, where the mobilization of bias results, as Schattschneider put it, from the form of organization. Of course, such collectivities and organizations are made up of individuals – but the power they exercise cannot be simply conceptualized in terms of individuals' decisions or behaviour. As Marx succinctly put it, 'Men make their own history but they do not make it just as they please; they do not make it under circumstances chosen by themselves, but under circumstances directly encountered, given and transmitted from the past.[8]

The second count on which the two-dimensional view of power is inadequate is in its association of power with actual, observable conflict. In this respect also the pluralists' critics follow their adversaries too closely[9] (and both in turn again follow Weber, who, as we have seen, stressed the realization of one's will, *despite the resistance of others*). This insistence on actual conflict as essential to power will not do, for at least two reasons.

The first is that, on Bachrach and Baratz's own analysis, two of the types of power may not involve such conflict: namely, manipulation and authority – which they conceive as 'agreement based upon reason' (Bachrach and Baratz 1970: 20), though elsewhere they speak of it as involving a 'possible conflict of values' (p. 37).

The second reason why the insistence on actual and observable conflict will not do is simply that it is highly unsatisfactory to suppose that power is only exercised in situations of such conflict. To put the matter sharply, *A* may exercise power over *B* by getting him to do what he does not want to do, but he also exercises power over him by influencing, shaping or determining his very wants. Indeed, is it not the supreme exercise of power to get another or others to have the desires you want them to have – that is, to secure their compliance by controlling their thoughts and desires? One does not have to go to the lengths of talking about *Brave New World*, or the world of B. F. Skinner, to see this: thought control takes many less total and more mundane forms, through the control of information, through the mass media and through the processes of socialization. Indeed, ironically, there are some excellent descriptions of this phenomenon in *Who Governs?* Consider the picture of the rule of the 'patricians' in the early nineteenth century: 'The elite seems to have possessed that most indispensable of all characteristics in a dominant group – the sense, shared not only by themselves but by the populace, that their claim to govern was legitimate' (Dahl 1961: 17). And Dahl also sees this phenomenon at work under modern 'pluralist' conditions: leaders, he says, 'do not merely *respond* to the preferences of constituents; leaders also *shape* preferences' (p. 164), and, again, 'almost the entire adult population has been subjected to *some* degree of indoctrination through the schools' (p. 317), etc. The trouble seems to be that both Bachrach and Baratz and the pluralists suppose that because power, as they conceptualize it, only shows up in cases of actual conflict, it follows that actual conflict is necessary to power. But this is to ignore the crucial point that the most effective and insidious use of power is to prevent such conflict from arising in the first place.

The third count on which the two-dimensional view of power is inadequate is closely linked to the second: namely, its insistence that nondecision-making power only exists where there are grievances which are denied entry into the political process in the form of issues. If the observer can uncover no grievances, then he must assume there is a 'genuine' consensus on the prevailing allocation of values. To put this another way, it is here assumed that if people feel no grievances, then they have no interests that are harmed by the use of power. But this is also highly unsatisfactory. In the first place, what, in any case, is a grievance – an articulated demand, based on political knowledge, an undirected complaint arising out of everyday experience, a vague feeling of unease or sense of deprivation? (See Lipsitz 1970.) Second, and more important, is it not the supreme and most insidious exercise of power to prevent people, to whatever degree, from having grievances by shaping their perceptions, cognitions and preferences in such a way that they accept their role in the existing order of things, either because they can see or imagine no alternative to it, or because they see it as natural and unchangeable, or because they value it as divinely ordained and beneficial? To assume that the absence of grievance equals genuine consensus is simply to rule out the possibility of false or manipulated consensus by definitional fiat.

In summary, the three-dimensional view of power involves a *thoroughgoing critique of the behavioural focus*[10] of the first two views as too individualistic and allows for consideration of the many ways in which *potential issues* are kept out of politics, whether through the operation of social forces and institutional practices or through individuals' decisions. This, moreover, can occur in the absence of actual, observable conflict, which may have been successfully averted – though there remains here an implicit reference to potential conflict. This potential, however, may never in fact be actualized. What one may have here is a *latent conflict*, which consists in a contradiction between the interests of those exercising power and the *real interests* of those they exclude.[11] These latter may not express or even be conscious of their interests, but, as I shall argue, the identification of those

28

interests ultimately always rests on empirically supportable and refutable hypotheses.

The distinctive features of the three views of power presented above are summarized below.

One-Dimensional View of Power

Focus on (a) behaviour
       (b) decision-making
       (c) (key) issues
       (d) observable (overt) conflict
       (e) (subjective) interests, seen as policy preferences revealed by political participation

Two-Dimensional View of Power

(Qualified) critique of behavioural focus
Focus on (a) decision-making and nondecision-making
       (b) issues and potential issues
       (c) observable (overt or covert) conflict
       (d) (subjective) interests, seen as policy preferences or grievances

Three-Dimensional View of Power

Critique of behavioural focus
Focus on (a) decision-making and control over political agenda (not necessarily through decisions)
       (b) issues and potential issues
       (c) observable (overt or covert), and latent conflict
       (d) subjective and real interests

5   The Underlying Concept of Power

One feature which these three views of power share is their evaluative character: each arises out of and operates within a particular moral and political perspective. Indeed, I maintain that power is one of those concepts which is ineradicably value-dependent. By this I mean that both its very definition and any given use of it, once defined, are inextricably tied to a given set of (probably unacknowledged) value-assumptions which predetermine the range of its empirical application – and I shall maintain below that some such uses permit that range to extend further and deeper than others. Moreover, the concept of power is, in consequence, what has been called an 'essentially contested concept' – one of those concepts which 'inevitably involve endless disputes about their proper uses on the part of their users' (Gallie 1955–6: 169). Indeed, to engage in such disputes is itself to engage in politics.

The absolutely basic common core to, or primitive notion lying behind, all talk of power is the notion that A in some way affects B. But, in applying that primitive (causal) notion to the analysis of social life, something further is needed – namely, the notion that A does so in a non-trivial or significant manner (see White 1972). Clearly, we all affect each other in countless ways all the time: the concept of power, and the related concepts of coercion, influence, authority, etc., pick out ranges of such affecting as being significant in specific ways. A way of conceiving power (or a way of defining the concept of power) that will be useful in the analysis of social relationships must imply an answer to the question: 'what counts as a significant manner?', 'what makes A's affecting B significant?' Now, the *concept* of power, thus defined, when interpreted and put to work, yields one or more *views* of power – that is, ways of identifying cases of power in the real world. The three views we have been considering can be seen as alternative interpretations and applications of one and the same underlying concept of power, according to which A exercises power over B when A affects B in a manner contrary to B's interests.[12] There are, however, alternative (no less contestable) ways of conceptualizing power, involving alternative criteria of significance. Let us look at two of them.

Consider, first, the concept of power elaborated by Talcott Parsons (1957, 1963a, 1963b, 1967). Parsons seeks to 'treat power as a *specific* mechanism operating to bring about changes in the action of other units, individual or collective, in the processes of social interaction' (1967: 299). What is it, in his view, that is specific about this mechanism, which distinguishes it as 'power'? In other words, what criteria of significance does Parsons use to identify a particular range of affecting as 'power'? The answer is, in a nutshell, the use of authoritative decisions to further collective goals. He defines power thus:

> Power then is generalized capacity to secure the performance of binding obligations by units in a system of collective organization when the obligations are legitimized with reference to their bearing on collective goals and where in case of recalcitrance there is a presumption of enforcement by negative situational sanctions – whatever the actual agency of that enforcement.   (p. 308)

The 'power of A over B is, in its legitimized form, the "right" of A, as a decision-making unit involved in collective process, to make decisions which take precedence over those of B, in the interest of the effectiveness of the collective operation as a whole' (p. 318).

Parsons's conceptualization of power ties it to authority, consensus and the pursuit of collective goals, and dissociates it from conflicts of interest and, in particular, from coercion and force. Thus power depends on 'the institutionalization of authority' (p. 331) and is 'conceived as a generalized medium of mobilizing commitments or obligation for effective collective action' (p. 331). By contrast, 'the threat of coercive measures, or of compulsion, without legitimation or justification, should not properly be called the use of power at all. . . .' (p. 331). Thus Parsons criticized Wright Mills for interpreting power 'exclusively as a facility for getting what one group, the holders of power, wants by preventing another group, the "outs", from getting what it wants', rather than seeing it as 'a facility for the performance of function in and on behalf of the society as a system' (Parsons 1957: 139).

Consider, secondly, the concept of power as defined by Hannah Arendt. 'Power', she writes,

> corresponds to the human ability not just to act but to act in concert. Power is never the property of an individual; it belongs to a group and remains in existence only so long as the group keeps together. When we say of somebody that he is 'in power' we actually refer to his being empowered by a certain number of people to act in their name. The moment the group, from which the power originated to begin with (*potestas in populo*, without a people or group there is no power), disappears, 'his power' also vanishes.   (Arendt 1970: 44)

It is

> the people's support that lends power to the institutions of a country, and this support is but the continuation of the consent that brought the laws into existence to begin with. Under conditions of representative government the people are supposed to rule those who govern them. All political institutions are manifestations and materializations of power; they petrify and decay as soon as the living power of the people ceases to uphold them. This is what Madison meant when he said 'all governments rest on opinion', a word no less true for the various forms of monarchy than for democracies.   (p. 41)

Arendt's way of conceiving power ties it to a tradition and a vocabulary which she traces back to Athens and Rome, according to which the republic is based on the rule of law, which rests on 'the power of the people' (p. 40). In this perspective power is dissociated from 'the command–obedience relationship' (p. 40) and 'the business of dominion' (p. 44). Power is consensual: it 'needs no justification, being inherent in the very existence of political communities; what it does need is legitimacy. . . . Power springs up whenever people get together and act in concert, but it derives its legitimacy from the initial getting together rather than from any action that then may follow' (p. 52). *Violence*, by contrast, is instrumental, a means to an end, but 'never will be legitimate' (p. 52). Power, 'far from being the means to an end, is actually the very condition enabling a group of people to think and act in terms of the means–end category' (p. 51).

The *point* of these rather similar definitions of power by Parsons and Arendt is to lend persuasive support to the general theoretical frameworks of their authors. In Parsons's case the linking of power to authoritative decisions and collective goals serves to reinforce his theory of social integration as based on value consensus by concealing from view the whole range of problems that have concerned so-called 'coercion' theorists, precisely under the rubric of 'power'. By definitional fiat, phenomena of coercion, exploitation, manipulation and so on cease to be phenomena of power – and in consequence disappear from the theoretical landscape. Anthony Giddens has put this point very well:

> Two obvious facts, that authoritative decisions very often do serve sectional interests and that the most radical conflicts in society stem from struggles for power, are defined out of consideration – at least as phenomena connected with 'power'. The conceptualisation of power which Parsons offers allows him to shift the entire weight of his analysis away from power as expressing a relation *between* individuals or groups, toward seeing power as a 'system property'. That collective 'goals', or even the values which lie behind them, may be the outcome of a 'negotiated order' built on conflicts between parties holding differential power is ignored, since for Parsons 'power' assumes the prior existence of collective goals. (Giddens 1968: 265)

In the case of Arendt, similarly, the conceptualization of power plays a persuasive role, in defence of her conception of 'the *res publica*, the public thing' to which people consent and 'behave nonviolently and argue rationally', and in opposition to the reduction of 'public affairs to the business of dominion' and to the conceptual linkage of power with force and violence. To 'speak of non-violent power', she writes, 'is actually redundant'

(Arendt 1970: 56). These distinctions enable Arendt to make statements such as the following: 'tyranny, as Montesquieu discovered, is therefore the most violent and least powerful of forms of government' (p. 41); 'Where power has disintegrated, revolutions are possible but not necessary' (p. 49); 'Even the most despotic domination we know of, the rule of master over slaves, who always outnumbered him, did not rest on superior means of coercion as such, but on a superior organization of power – that is, on the organized solidarity of the masters' (p. 50); 'Violence can always destroy power; out of the barrel of a gun grows the most effective command, resulting in the most instant and perfect obedience. What can never grow out of it is power' (p. 53); 'Power and violence are opposites; where the one rules absolutely, the other is absent. Violence appears where power is in jeopardy, but left to its own course it ends in power's disappearance' (p. 56).

These conceptualizations of power are rationally defensible. It is, however, the contention of this book that they are of less value than that advanced here for two reasons.

In the first place, they are revisionary persuasive redefinitions of power which are out of line with the central meanings of 'power' as traditionally understood and with the concerns that have always centrally preoccupied students of power. They focus on the locution 'power to', ignoring 'power over'. Thus power indicates a 'capacity', a 'facility', an 'ability', not a relationship. Accordingly, the conflictual aspect of power – the fact that it is exercised *over* people – disappears altogether from view.[13] And along with it there disappears the central interest of studying power relations in the first place – an interest in the (attempted or successful) securing of people's compliance by overcoming or averting their opposition.

In the second place, the point of these definitions is, as we have seen, to reinforce certain theoretical positions; but everything that can be said by their means can be said with greater clarity by means of the conceptual scheme here proposed, without thereby concealing from view the (central) aspects of power which they define out of existence. Thus, for instance, Parsons objects to seeing power as a 'zero-sum' phenomenon and appeals to the analogy of credit creation in the economy, arguing that the use of power, as when the ruled have justified confidence in their rulers, may achieve objectives which all desire and from which all benefit. It has been argued in defence of this view that 'in any type of group, the existence of defined "leadership" positions does "generate" power which may be used to achieve aims desired by the majority of the members of the group' (Giddens 1968: 263). Similarly, Arendt wants to say that members of a group acting in concert are exercising power. According to the conceptual scheme here advanced, all such cases of co-operative activity, where individuals or groups significantly affect one another in the absence of a conflict of interests between them, will be identifiable, as cases of 'influence' but not of 'power'. All that Parsons and Arendt wish to say about consensual behaviour remains sayable, but so also does all that they wish to remove from the language of power.

It may be useful if at this point I set out a conceptual map (Figure 1) of power and its cognates (all modes of 'significant affecting') – a map which broadly follows Bachrach and Baratz's typology, referred to above. Needless to say, this map is itself essentially contestable – and, in particular, although it is meant to analyse and situate the concept of power which underlies the one-, two- and three-dimensional views of power, I do not claim that it would necessarily be acceptable to all the proponents of those respective views. One reason for that, of course, is that it is developed from the perspective of the three-dimensional view, which incorporates and therefore goes further than the other two.

It will be seen that in this scheme power may or may not be a form of influence – depending on whether sanctions are involved; while influence and authority may or may not be a form of power – depending on whether a conflict of interests is involved. Consensual authority, with no conflict of interests, is not, therefore, a form of power.

The question of whether rational persuasion is a form of power and influence cannot be adequately treated here. For what it is

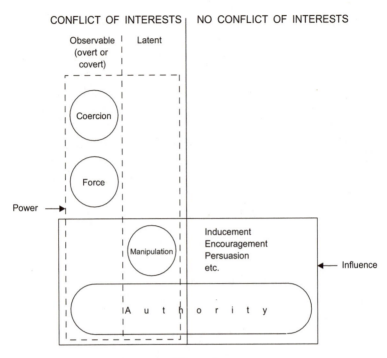

Figure 1

worth, my inclination is to say both yes and no. Yes, because it is a form of significant affecting: *A* gets (causes) *B* to do or think what he would not otherwise do or think. No, because *B* autonomously accepts *A*'s reasons, so that one is inclined to say that it is not *A* but *A*'s reasons, or *B*'s acceptance of them, that is responsible for *B*'s change of course. I suspect that we are here in the presence of a fundamental (Kantian) antinomy between causality, on the one hand, and autonomy and reason, on the other. I see no way of resolving this antinomy: there are simply contradictory conceptual pressures at work.

It may further be asked whether power can be exercised by *A* over *B* in *B*'s real interests. That is, suppose there is a conflict now between the preferences of *A* and *B*, but that *A*'s preferences are in *B*'s real interests. To this there are two possible responses: (1) that *A* might exercise 'short-term power' over *B* (with an observable conflict of subjective interests), but that if and when *B* recognizes his real interests, the power relation ends: it is self-annihilating; or (2) that all or most forms of attempted or successful control by *A* over *B*, when *B* objects or resists, constitute a violation of *B*'s autonomy; that *B* has a real interest in his own autonomy; so that such an exercise of power cannot be in *B*'s real interests. Clearly the first of these responses is open to misuse by seeming to provide a paternalist licence for tyranny; while the second furnishes an anarchist defence against it, collapsing all or most cases of influence into power. Though attracted by the second, I am inclined to adopt the first, the dangers of which may be obviated by insisting on the empirical basis for identifying real interests. The identification of these is not up to *A*, *but to B*, exercising choice under conditions of relative autonomy and, in particular, independently of *A*'s power (e.g. through democratic participation).[14]

6 Power and Interests

I have defined the concept of power by saying that *A* exercises power over *B* when *A* affects *B* in a manner contrary to *B*'s interests. Now the notion of 'interests' is an irreducibly evaluative notion (Balbus 1971, Connolly 1972): if I say that something is in your interests, I imply that you have a prima facie claim to it, and if I say that 'policy *x* is in *A*'s interest' this constitutes a prima facie justification for that policy. In general, talk of interests provides a licence for the making of normative judgments of a moral and political character. So it is not surprising that different conceptions of what interests *are* are associated with different moral and political positions. Extremely crudely, one might say that the liberal takes people as they are and applies want-regarding principles to them, relating their interests to what they actually want or prefer, to their policy preferences as manifested by their political participation.[15] The reformist, seeing and deploring that not everyone's wants are given equal weight by the political system, also relates their interests to what they want or prefer, but allows that this may be revealed in more indirect and sub-political ways – in the form of deflected, submerged or concealed wants and preferences. The radical, however, maintains that people's wants may themselves be a product of a system which works against their interests, and, in such cases, relates the latter to what they would want and prefer, were they able to make the choice.[16] Each of these three picks out a certain range of the entire class of actual and potential wants as the relevant object of moral appraisal. In brief, my suggestion is that the one-dimensional view of power presupposes a liberal conception of interests, the two-dimensional view a reformist conception, and the three-dimensional view a radical conception. (And I would maintain that any view of power rests on some normatively specific conception of interests.)

7   The Three Views Compared

I now turn to consider the relative strengths and weaknesses of the three views of power I have outlined.

The virtues of the decision-making or one-dimensional view are obvious and have often been stressed: by means of it, to cite Merelman again, the pluralists 'studied actual behavior, stressed operational definitions, and turned up evidence' (Merelman 1968a: 451). However, the trouble is that, by doing this, by studying the making of important decisions within the community, they were simply taking over and reproducing the bias of the system they were studying. By analysing the decisions on urban redevelopment, public education and political nominations, Dahl tells us a good deal about the *diversity* of decision-making power in New Haven. He shows that these issue areas are independent of one another, and that, by and large, different individuals exercise power in different areas and therefore no set of individuals and thus no single elite has decision-making power ranging across different issue areas. He further argues that the decision-making process is responsive to the preferences of citizens because the elected politicians and officials engaged in it anticipate the results of future elections. It would, he writes, 'be unwise to underestimate the extent to which voters may exert *indirect* influence on the decisions of leaders by means of elections (Dahl 1961: 101): no issue of importance to the former is likely to be ignored for long by the latter. Thus Dahl pictures pluralist politics as both diverse and open: he writes, '[T]he independence, penetrability, and heterogeneity of the various segments of the political stratum all but guarantee that any dissatisfied group will find spokesmen in the political stratum' (p. 93). But the diversity and openness Dahl sees may be highly misleading if power is being exercised within the system to limit decision-making to acceptable issues. Individuals and elites may act separately in making acceptable decisions, but they may act in concert – or even fail to act at all – in such a way as to keep unacceptable issues out of politics, thereby preventing the system from becoming any more diverse than it is. 'A polity', it has been suggested, 'that is pluralistic in its decision-making can be unified in its non-decision-making' (Crenson 1971: 179). The decision-making method prevents this possibility from being considered. Dahl concludes that the system is penetrable by any dissatisfied group, but he does so only by studying cases of successful penetration, and never examines failed attempts at such penetration. Moreover, the thesis that indirect influence gives the electorate control over leaders can be turned on its head. Indirect influence can equally operate to prevent politicians, officials or others from raising issues or proposals known to be unacceptable to some group or institution in the community. It can serve the interests of an elite, not only that of the electorate. In brief, the one-dimensional view of power cannot reveal the less visible ways in which a pluralist system may be biased in favour of certain groups and against others.

The two-dimensional view goes some way to revealing this which is a considerable advance in itself – but it confines itself to studying situations where the mobilization of bias can be attributed to individuals' decisions that have the effect of preventing currently observable grievances (overt or covert) from becoming issues within the political process. This, I think, largely accounts for the very thin and inadequate character of Bachrach and Bar-atz's study of poverty, race and politics in Baltimore. All that study really amounts to is an account of various decisions by the mayor and various business leaders to deflect the inchoate demands of Baltimore's blacks from becoming politically threatening issues – by such devices as making certain appointments, establishing task forces to defuse the poverty issue, by supporting certain kinds of welfare measures, etc. – together with an account of how the blacks gained political access through overt struggle involving riots. The analysis remains superficial precisely because it confines itself to studying individual decisions made to avert potentially threatening demands from becoming politically dangerous. A deeper analysis would also concern itself with all the complex and subtle ways in which the *inactivity* of leaders and the sheer weight of institutions – political, industrial and educational – served for so long to keep the blacks out of Baltimore politics; and indeed for a long period kept them from even trying to get into it.

The three-dimensional view offers the possibility of such an analysis. It offers, in other words, the prospect of a serious socio-logical and not merely personalized explanation of how political systems prevent demands from becoming political issues or even from being made. Now the classical objection to doing this has often been stated by pluralists: how can one study, let alone explain, what does not happen? Polsby writes:

> it has been suggested that non-events make more significant policy than do policy-making events. This is the kind of statement that has a certain plausibility and attractiveness but that presents truly insuperable obstacles to research. We can sound the depth of the abyss very quickly by agreeing that non-events are much more important than events, and inquiring precisely *which* non-events are to be regarded as most significant in the community. Surely not *all* of them. For every event (no matter how defined) that occurs there must be an infinity of alternatives. Then which non-events are to be regarded as significant? One satisfactory answer might be: those outcomes

40

desired by a significant number of actors in the community but not achieved. Insofar as these goals are in some way explicitly pursued by people in the community, the method of study used in New Haven has a reasonable chance of capturing them. A wholly unsatisfactory answer would be: certain non-events stipulated by outside observers without reference to the desires or activities of community residents. The answer is unsatisfactory because it is obviously inappropriate for outsiders to pick among all the possible outcomes that did not take place a set which they regard as important but which community citizens do not. This approach is likely to prejudice the outcomes of research. . . .   (Polsby 1963: 96–7)

Similarly, Wolfinger argues that the 'infinite variety of possible nondecisions . . . reveals the idea's adaptability to various ideological perspectives' (Wolfinger 1971a: 1078). Moreover, suppose we advance 'a theory of political interests and rational behavior' specifying how people would behave in certain situations if left to themselves, and use it to support the claim that their failure so to behave is due to the exercise of power. In this case, Wolfinger argues, we have no means of deciding between two possibilities: either that there was an exercise of power, or that the theory was wrong (p. 1078).

The first point to be made against these apparently powerful arguments is that they move from a methodological difficulty to a substantive assertion. It does not follow that, just because it is difficult or even impossible to show that power has been exercised in a given situation, we can conclude that it has not. But, more importantly, I do not believe that it is impossible to identify an exercise of power of this type.

What is an exercise of power? What is it to exercise power? On close inspection it turns out that the locution 'exercise of power' and 'exercising power' is problematic in at least two ways.

In the first place, it carries, in everyday usage, a doubly unfortunate connotation: it is sometimes assumed to be both individualistic and intentional, that is, it seems to carry the suggestion that the exercise of power is a matter of individuals

41

consciously acting to affect others. Some appear to feel discomfort in speaking either of groups, institutions, or collectivities 'exercising' power, or of individuals or collectivities doing so unconsciously. This is an interesting case of individualistic and intentional assumptions being built into our language – but that in itself provides no reason for adopting such assumptions. In what follows I propose to abandon these assumptions and to speak of the exercise of power whether by individuals or by groups, institutions, etc., and whether consciously or not. A negative justification for this revisionary usage is that there is no other available word that meets the bill (thus 'exerting' power is little different from 'exercising' it); I shall offer a positive justification below.

The second way in which the phrase 'exercising power' is problematic is that it conceals an interesting and important ambiguity. I referred above to Dahl's definition of the exercise of power in terms of A getting B to do something he would not otherwise do. However, this is, as it stands, too simple.

Suppose that A can *normally* affect B. This is to suppose that, against the background of (what is assumed to be) a normally ongoing situation, if A does x, he gets B to do what he would not otherwise do. Here A's action, x, is *sufficient* to get B to do what he would not otherwise do. Suppose, however, that exactly the same is true of A_1. He can also normally affect B: his action, y, is also sufficient to get B to do what he would not otherwise do, in just the same way. Now, suppose that A and A_1 both act in relation to B simultaneously and B changes his action accordingly. Here, it is clear, B's action or change of course is overdetermined: both A and A_1 have affected B by 'exercising power', but the result is the same as that which would have occurred had either affected him singly. In this case it is a pointless question to ask which of them produced the change of course, that is, which of them made a difference to the result: they both did. They both 'exercised power', in a sense – that is, a power *sufficient* to produce the result, yet one cannot say that *either* of them made a difference to the result. Let us call this sense of 'exercising power' the *operative* sense.

Contrast this case with the case where *A does* make a difference to the result: that is, against the background of a normally
ongoing situation, *A*, by doing *x*, actually gets *B* to do what *B*
would not otherwise do. Here *x* is an intervening cause which
distorts the normal course of events – by contrast with the first,
overdetermined case, where there are, *ex hypothesi, two* intervening sufficient conditions, so that neither can be said to have 'made
a difference', just because of the presence of the other: there the
normal course of events is itself distorted by the presence of
the other intervening sufficient condition. Here, by contrast, *A*'s
intervention can be said to make a difference to the result. Let us
call this sense of 'exercising power' the *effective* sense.

(It is worth adding a further distinction, which turns on *what*
difference *A* makes to the result. *A* wishes *B* to do some particular
thing, but, in exercising effective power over him, he may succeed in changing *B*'s course in a wide variety of ways. Only in
the case where *B*'s change of course corresponds to *A*'s wishes,
that is, where *A* secures *B*'s compliance, can we speak properly
of a *successful* exercise of power: here 'affecting' becomes 'control'. It is, incidentally, this case of the successful exercise of
power, or the securing of compliance, on which Bachrach and
Baratz exclusively concentrate. The successful exercise of power
can be seen as a sub-species of the effective exercise of power –
though one could maintain that, where the operative exercise of
power issues in compliance, this also is an [indeterminate] form
of its successful exercise.)

We can now turn to the analysis of what exactly is involved in
identifying an exercise of power. An attribution of the exercise of
power involves, among other things, the double claim that *A* acts
(or fails to act) in a certain way and that *B* does what he would
not otherwise do (I use the term 'do' here in a very wide sense,
to include 'think', 'want', 'feel', etc.). In the case of an effective
exercise of power, *A* gets *B* to do what he would not otherwise do;
in the case of an operative exercise of power, *A*, together with
another or other sufficient conditions, gets *B* to do what he
would not otherwise do. Hence, in general, any attribution of
the exercise of power (including, of course, those by Dahl and

his colleagues) always implies a relevant counterfactual, to the effect that (but for A, or but for A together with any other sufficient conditions) B would otherwise have done, let us say, b. This is one reason why so many thinkers (mistakenly) insist on actual, observable conflict as essential to power (though there are doubtless other theoretical and, indeed, ideological reasons). For such conflict provides the relevant counterfactual, so to speak, ready-made. If A and B are in conflict with one another, A wanting a and B wanting b, then if A prevails over B, we can assume that B would otherwise have done b. Where there is no observable conflict between A and B, then we must provide other grounds for asserting the relevant counterfactual. That is, we must provide other, indirect, grounds for asserting that if A had not acted (or failed to act) in a certain way – and, in the case of operative power, if other sufficient conditions had not been operative – then B would have thought and acted differently from the way he does actually think and act. In brief, we need to justify our expectation that B would have thought or acted differently; and we also need to specify the means or mechanism by which A has prevented, or else acted (or abstained from acting) in a manner sufficient to prevent, B from doing so.

I can see no reason to suppose that either of these claims cannot in principle be supported – though I do not claim it is easy. Doing so certainly requires one to go much deeper than most analyses of power in contemporary political science and sociology. Fortunately, Matthew Crenson's book *The Un-Politics of Air Pollution: A Study of Non-Decisionmaking in the Cities* (Crenson 1971) provides a good example of how the task can be approached. The theoretical framework of this book can be seen as lying on the borderline of the two-dimensional and the three-dimensional views of power: I see it as a serious attempt empirically to apply the former, together with certain elements of the latter. For that reason, it marks a real theoretical advance in the empirical study of power relations.

It explicitly attempts to find a way to explain 'things that do not happen', on the assumption that 'the proper object of

investigation is not political activity but political inactivity'
(pp. vii, 26). Why, he asks, was the issue of air pollution not
raised as early or as effectively in some American cities as it was
in others? His object, in other words, is to 'discover ... why many
cities and towns in the United States failed to make a political
issue of their air pollution problems' (p. vii), thereby illuminating the character of local political systems – particularly with
respect to their 'penetrability'. He first shows that differences in
the treatment of pollution cannot be attributed solely to differences in the actual pollution level or to social characteristics of
the populations in question. He then provides a detailed study
of two neighbouring cities in Indiana, both equally polluted
and with similar populations, one of which, East Chicago, took
action to clear its air in 1949, while the other, Gary, held its
breath until 1962. Briefly, his explanation of the difference is
that Gary is a one-company town dominated by US Steel, with
a strong party organization, whereas East Chicago had a number of steel companies and no strong party organization when it
passed its air pollution control ordinance.

His case (which he documents with convincing detail) is that
US Steel, which had built Gary and was responsible for its pros-
perity, for a long time effectively prevented the issue from even
being raised, through its power reputation operating on anticipated reactions, then for a number of years thwarted attempts to
raise the issue, and decisively influenced the content of the anti-
pollution ordinance finally enacted. Moreover, it did all this
without acting or entering into the political arena. Its 'mere
reputation for power, unsupported by acts of power' was 'sufficient to inhibit the emergence of the dirty air issue' (p. 124); and,
when it eventually did emerge (largely because of the threat of
Federal or State action), 'US Steel ... influenced the content
of the pollution ordinance without taking any action on it, and
thus defied the pluralist dictum that political power belongs
to political actors' (pp. 69–70). US Steel, Crenson argues, exercised influence 'from points outside the range of observable
political behaviour. ... Though the corporation seldom inter-
vened directly in the deliberations of the town's air pollution

policymakers, it was nevertheless able to affect their scope and direction' (p. 107). He writes:

> Gary's anti-pollution activists were long unable to get US Steel to take a clear stand. One of them, looking back on the bleak days of the dirty air debate, cited the evasiveness of the town's largest industrial corporation as a decisive factor in frustrating early efforts to enact a pollution control ordinance. The company executives, he said, would just nod sympathetically 'and agree that air pollution was terrible, and pat you on the head. But they never *did* anything one way or the other. If only there had been a fight, then something might have been accomplished!' What US Steel did not do was probably more important to the career of Gary's air pollution issue than what it did do.   (pp. 76–7)

He then moves from these two detailed case studies to a comparative analysis of interview data with political leaders taken from 51 cities, aimed at testing the hypotheses arising out of the two case studies. Briefly, his conclusions are that 'the air pollution issue tends not to flourish in cities where industry enjoys a reputation for power' (p. 145) – and that 'where industry remains silent about dirty air, the life chances of the pollution issue are likely to be diminished' (p. 124). Again, a strong and influential party organization will also inhibit the growth of the pollution issue, since demands for clean air are unlikely to yield the kind of specific benefits that American party machines seek – though where industry has a high power reputation, a strong party will increase the pollution issue's life chances, since it will seek to purchase industrial influence. In general Crenson plausibly argues that pollution control is a good example of a collective good, whose specific costs are concentrated on industry: thus the latter's opposition will be strong, while the support for it will be relatively weak, since its benefits are diffuse and likely to have little appeal to party leaders engaged in influence brokerage. Moreover, and very interestingly, Crenson argues, against the pluralists, that political issues tend to be interconnected; and thus collective issues tend to promote other collective issues, and vice versa. Thus by 'promoting one political agenda item, civic activists may succeed in driving other issues away' (p. 170):

> where business and industrial development is a topic of local concern, the dirty air problem tends to be ignored. The prominence of one issue appears to be connected with the subordination of the other, and the existence of this connection calls into question the pluralist view that different political issues tend to rise and subside independently.   (p. 165)

Crenson's general case is that there are 'politically imposed limitations upon the scope of decision-making', such that 'decision-making activity is channelled and directed by the process of non-decision-making' (p. 178). Pluralism, in other words, is 'no guarantee of political openness or popular sovereignty'; and neither the study of decision-making nor the existence of 'visible diversity' will tell us anything about 'those groups and issues which may have been shut out of a town's political life' (p. 181).

I suggested above that the theoretical framework of Crenson's analysis lies on the borderline of the two-dimensional and the three-dimensional views of power. It is, on the face of it, a two-dimensional study of nondecision-making *à la* Bachrach and Baratz. On the other hand, it begins to advance beyond their position (as presented in their book) in three ways. First, it does not interpret nondecision-making behaviourally, as exhibited only in decisions (hence the stress on inaction – 'What US Steel did not do . . .'); second, it is non-individualistic and considers institutional power;[17] and third, it considers ways in which demands are prevented, through the exercise of such power, from being raised: thus,

> Local political forms and practices may even inhibit citizens' ability to transform some diffuse discontent into an explicit demand. In short, there is something like an inarticulate ideology in political institutions, even in those that appear to be most open-minded, flexible and disjointed – an ideology in

the sense that it promotes the selective perception and articulation of social problems and conflicts. ....   (p. 23)

In this way, 'local political institutions and political leaders
may . . . exercise considerable control over what people choose to
care about and how forcefully they articulate their cares' (p. 27):
restrictions on the scope of decision-making may 'stunt the
political consciousness of the local public' by confining minority
opinions to minorities and denying 'minorities the opportunity
to grow to majorities' (pp. 180–1).

Crenson's analysis is impressive because it fulfils the double
requirement mentioned above: there is good reason to expect
that, other things being equal, people would rather not be
poisoned (assuming, in particular, that pollution control does
not necessarily mean unemployment) – even where they may
not even articulate this preference; and hard evidence is given
of the ways in which institutions, specifically US Steel, largely
through inaction, prevented the citizens' interest in not being
poisoned from being acted on (though other factors, institutional
and ideological, would need to enter a fuller explanation). Thus
both the relevant counterfactual and the identification of a
power mechanism are justified.

8 Difficulties

I wish, however, to conclude on a problematic note, by allud-
ing to the difficulties, peculiar to the three-dimensional view
of power, first, of justifying the relevant counterfactual, and
second, of identifying the mechanism or process of an alleged
exercise of power.

In the first place, justifying the relevant counterfactual is not
always as easy or as clearcut as in the case of air pollution in
Gary, Indiana. There are a number of features of that case that
may not be present in others. First, the value judgement implicit
in the specification of Gary's citizens' interest in not being

poisoned is scarcely disputable – resting, as Crenson says, on 'the opinion of the observer concerning the value of human life' (p. 3). Second, the empirical hypothesis that those citizens, if they had the choice and fuller information, would prefer not to be poisoned is more than plausible (on the assumption that such an alternative did not entail increased unemployment). And third, Crenson's study provides comparative data to support the claim that, under different conditions where the alleged nondecisional power was not operative, or operative to a lesser degree, people with comparable social characteristics did make and enforce that choice, or did so with less difficulty.[18]

Sometimes, however, it is extraordinarily difficult to justify the relevant counterfactual. Can we always assume that the victims of injustice and inequality would, but for the exercise of power, strive for justice and equality? What about the cultural relativity of values? Is not such an assumption a form of ethnocentrism? Why not say that acquiescence in a value system 'we' reject, such as orthodox communism or the caste system, is a case of genuine consensus over different values? But even here empirical support is not beyond our reach. It is not impossible to adduce evidence – which must, by nature of the case, be indirect – to support the claim that an apparent case of consensus is not genuine but imposed (though there will be mixed cases, with respect to different groups and different components of the value system).

Where is such evidence to be found? There is a most interesting passage in Antonio Gramsci's *Prison Notebooks* which bears on this question, where Gramsci draws a contrast between 'thought and action, i.e. the co-existence of two conceptions of the world, one affirmed in words and the other displayed in effective action' (Gramsci 1971[1926–37]: 326). Where this contrast occurs 'in the life of great masses', Gramsci writes, it

> cannot but be the expression of profounder contrasts of a social historical order. It signifies that the social group in question may indeed have its own conception of the world, even if only embryonic; a conception which manifests itself in action, but

occasionally and in flashes – when, that is, the group is acting as an organic totality. But this same group has, for reasons of submission and intellectual subordination, adopted a conception which is not its own but is borrowed from another group; and it affirms this conception verbally and believes itself to be following it, because this is the conception which it follows in 'normal times' – that is when its conduct is not independent and autonomous, but submissive and subordinate.   (p. 327)[19]

Although one may not accept Gramsci's attribution of 'its own conception of the world' to a social group, it can be highly instructive (though not conclusive) to observe how people behave in 'abnormal times' – when (*ex hypothesi*) 'submission and intellectual subordination' are absent or diminished, when the apparatus of power is removed or relaxed. Gramsci himself gives the example of 'the fortunes of religions and churches':

Religion, or a particular church, maintains its community of faithful (within the limits imposed by the necessities of general historical development) in so far as it nourishes its faith permanently and in an organized fashion, indefatigably repeating its apologetics, struggling at all times and always with the same kind of arguments, and maintaining a hierarchy of intellectuals who give to the faith, in appearance at least, the dignity of thought. Whenever the continuity of relations between the Church and the faithful has been violently interrupted, for political reasons, as happened during the French Revolution, the losses suffered by the Church have been incalculable.   (p. 340)

As a contemporary example, consider the reactions of Czechs to the relaxation of the apparatus of power in 1968.

But evidence can also be sought in 'normal times'. We are concerned to find out what the exercise of power prevents people from doing, and sometimes even thinking. Hence we should examine how people react to opportunities – or, more precisely, perceived opportunities – when these occur, to escape from subordinate positions in hierarchical systems. In this connection data about rates of social mobility can acquire a new and striking theoretical significance. The caste system is often thought of as a plausible candidate for 'a case of genuine consensus over different values'. But the whole recent debate over 'Sanskritization' suggests otherwise. The caste system, according to Srinivas,

> is far from a rigid system in which the position of each component caste is fixed for all time. Movement has always been possible, and especially so in the middle regions of the hierarchy. A low caste was able, in a generation or two, to rise to a higher position in the hierarchy by adopting vegetarianism and teetotalism, and by Sanskritizing its ritual and pantheon. In short, it took over, as far as possible, the customs, rites and beliefs of the Brahmins, and the adoption of the Brahminic way of life by a low caste seems to have been frequent, though theoretically forbidden. This process has been called 'Sanskritization'.   (Srinivas 1952: 30)

Srinivas argues that 'economic betterment ... seems to lead to the Sanskritization of the customs and way of life of a group', which itself depends on 'the collective desire to rise high in the esteem of friends, neighbours and rivals' and is followed by 'the adoption of methods by which the status of the group is raised' (Srinivas 1962: 56–7). Such a desire is, it seems, usually preceded by the acquisition of wealth, but the acquisition of political power, education and leadership also seems to be relevant. In brief, the evidence suggests that there is a significant difference between the caste system as it exists in the 'popular conception' and as it actually operates (Srinivas 1962: 56). What to the outside observer may appear as a value consensus which sanctifies an extreme, elaborately precise and stable hierarchy actually conceals the fact that perceived opportunities of lower castes to rise within the system are very often, if not invariably, seized.

It could be argued that this is not a very persuasive case, since upward mobility within a hierarchical system implies acceptance of the hierarchy, so that the Sanskritizing castes are not rejecting but embracing the value system. But against this it can be objected that this is precisely a case of a gap between thought and action, since the adoption of the Brahminic way of life by a low caste is theoretically forbidden and in general caste position is held to be ascriptive, hereditary and unchangeable.

Other, less ambiguous, evidence relating to the Indian caste system can, however, be adduced which supports the claim that the internalization of subordinate status is a consequence of power. Consider the effects of the introduction of universal suffrage upon lower castes' acceptance of the principle of hierarchy.[20] More tellingly still, consider the 'ways out' taken by the Untouchables, above all that of mass conversion into other religions.[21] At various periods in their history, the Untouchables have embraced Islam,[22] Christianity and Buddhism,[23] because they proclaimed egalitarian principles and offered the hope of escape from caste discrimination.[24]

I conclude, then, that, in general, evidence can be adduced (though by nature of the case, such evidence will never be conclusive) which supports the relevant counterfactuals implicit in identifying exercises of power of the three-dimensional type. One can take steps to find out what it is that people would have done otherwise.

How, in the second place, is one to identify the process or mechanism of an alleged exercise of power, on the three-dimensional view? (I shall leave aside the further problems of identifying an operative exercise of power, that is, the problem of overdetermination. That is a whole issue in itself.) There are three features, distinctive of the three-dimensional view, which pose peculiarly acute problems for the researcher. As I have argued, such an exercise may, in the first place, involve inaction rather than (observable) action. In the second place, it may be unconscious (this seems to be allowed for on the two-dimensional view, but the latter also insists that nondecisions are *decisions* – and, in the absence of further explanation, an unconscious decision looks like a contradiction). And in the third place, power may be exercised by collectivities, such as groups or institutions. Let us examine these difficulties in turn.

First, inaction. Here, once more, we have a non-event. Indeed, where the suppression of a potential issue is attributed to inaction, we have a *double* non-event. How can such a situation be identified empirically? The first step to answering this is to see that inaction need not be a featureless non-event. The failure to act in a certain way, in a given situation, may well have specifiable consequences, where acting in that way is a hypothesised possibility with determinate consequences. Moreover, the consequence of inaction may well be a further non-event, such as the non-appearance of a political issue, where the actions in question would, *ex hypothesi*, have led to its appearance. There seems to be no impossibility in principle of establishing a causal nexus here: the relation between the inaction of US Steel and the public silence over air pollution is an admirable case in point.

Second, unconsciousness. How can power be exercised without the exerciser being aware of what he (it) is doing? Here it will be useful to make a number of distinctions (and, for brevity, in what follows I use the term 'action' to cover the case of inaction). There are a number of ways of being unconscious of what one is doing. One may be unaware of what is held to be the 'real' motive or meaning of one's action (as in standard Freudian cases). Or, second, one may be unaware of how others interpret one's action. Or, third, one may be unaware of the consequences of one's action. Identifying an unconscious exercise of power of the first type presents the usual difficulty, characteristic of Freudian-type explanations, of establishing the 'real' motive or meaning, where the interpretations of observer and observed differ. This difficulty, however, is well known and has been very widely discussed, and it is not peculiar to the analysis of power. Identifying an unconscious exercise of power of the second type seems to pose no particular problem. It is the third type which is really problematic, in cases where the agent *could not be expected* to have knowledge of the consequences of his action. Can *A* properly be said to exercise power over *B* where knowledge of the effects of *A* upon *B* is just not available to *A*? If *A*'s ignorance of those effects is due to his (remediable) failure to find out, the answer appears to be yes. Where, however, he could not have found out – because, say, certain factual or technical knowledge was simply not *available* – then talk of an exercise of power appears to lose all its point. Consider, for instance, the case of a drug company which allegedly exercises the most extreme power – of life and death – over members of the public by marketing a dangerous drug. Here the allegation that power is being exercised is not refuted if it could be shown that the company's scientists and managers did not know that the drug's effects were dangerous: they could have taken steps to find out. On the other hand, did cigarette companies exercise this power over the public before it was even supposed that cigarette smoking might be harmful? Surely not. This suggests that where power is held to be exercised unconsciously in this sense (i.e. in unawareness of its consequences), the assumption is being made that the exerciser or exercisers could, in the context, have ascertained those consequences. (Of course, justifying that assumption raises further problems, since it involves, for example, the making of historical judgments about the locus of culturally determined limits to cognitive innovation.)

The third difficulty is that of attributing an exercise of power to collectivities, such as groups, classes or institutions. The problem is: when can social causation be characterized as an exercise of power, or, more precisely, how and where is the line to be drawn between structural determination, on the one hand, and an exercise of power, on the other? This is a problem which has often reappeared in the history of Marxist thought, in the context of discussions of determinism and voluntarism. Thus, for example, within post-war French Marxism, an extreme determinist position was adopted by the structuralist Marxism of Louis Althusser and his followers, as opposed to the so-called 'humanist', 'historicist' and 'subjectivist' interpretations of thinkers such as Sartre and Lucien Goldmann, and behind them of Lukács and Korsch (and, behind them, of Hegel) for whom the historical 'subject' has a crucial and ineradicable explanatory role. For Althusser, Marx's thought, properly understood, conceptualizes 'the determination of the elements of a whole by the structure of the whole', and 'liberated definitively from the empiricist antinomies of phenomenal subjectivity and essential interiority', treats of 'an objective system governed, in its most concrete determinations, by the laws of its *arrangement (montage)* and of its *machinery*, by the specifications of its concept' (Althusser and Balibar 1968, ii: 63, 71).

The implications of this position can be seen very clearly in the debate between the Althusserian Nicos Poulantzas, and the British political sociologist Ralph Miliband, over the latter's book *The State in Capitalist Society* (Miliband 1969). According to Poulantzas, Miliband had

> difficulties ... in comprehending social classes and the State as *objective structures*, and their relations as an *objective system of regular connections*, a structure and a system whose agents, 'men', are in the words of Marx, 'bearers' of it – *träger*. Miliband constantly gives the impression that for him social classes or 'groups' are in some way reducible to *inter-personal relations*, that the State is reducible to inter-personal relations of the members of the diverse 'groups' that constitute the State apparatus, and finally that the relation between social classes and the State is itself reducible to inter-personal relations of 'individuals' composing social groups and 'individuals' composing the State apparatus.   (Poulantzas 1969: 70)

This conception, Poulantzas continued,

> seems to me to derive from a *problematic of the subject* which has had constant repercussions in the history of Marxist thought. According to this problematic, the agents of a social formation, 'men', are not considered as the 'bearers' of objective instances (as they are for Marx), but as the genetic principle of the levels of the social whole. This is a problematic of *social actors*, of individuals as the origin of *social action*: sociological research thus leads finally not to the study of the objective co-ordinates that determine the distribution of agents into social classes and the contradictions between these classes, but to the search for *finalist* explanations founded on the *motivations of conduct* of the individual actors.   (p. 70)

Miliband, in response to this, maintained that Poulantzas

> is here rather one-sided and that he goes much too far in dismissing the nature of the state elite as of altogether no account. For what his *exclusive* stress on 'objective relations' suggests is that what the state does is in every particular and at all times *wholly* determined by these 'objective relations': in other words, that the structural constraints of the system are so absolutely compelling as to turn those who run the state into the merest functionaries and executants of policies imposed upon them by 'the system'. (Miliband 1970: 57)

Poulantzas, wrote Miliband, substituted 'the notion of "objective structures" and "objective relations" for the notion of a "ruling" class', and his analysis leads 'straight towards a kind of structural determinism, or rather a structural super-determinism, which makes impossible a truly realistic consideration of the dialectical relationship between the State and "the system"' (p. 57).[25]

The first thing to say about this debate is that Poulantzas's implied dichotomy between structural determinism and methodological individualism – between his own 'problematic' and that of '*social actors*, of individuals as the origin of social action' – is misleading. These are not the only two possibilities. It is not a question of sociological research 'leading finally' *either* to the study of 'objective co-ordinates' *or* to that of 'motivations of conduct of the individual actors'. Such research must clearly examine the complex interrelations between the two, and allow for the obvious fact that individuals act together and upon one another within groups and organisations, and that the explanation of their behaviour and interaction is unlikely to be reducible merely to their individual motivations.

The second thing to say about the Poulantzas–Miliband debate is that it turns on a crucially important conceptual distinction – which the language of power serves to mark out. To use the vocabulary of power in the context of social relationships is to speak of human agents, separately or together, in groups or organisations, through action or inaction, significantly affecting the thoughts or actions of others (specifically, in a manner contrary to their interests). In speaking thus, one assumes that, although the agents operate within structurally determined limits, they none the less have a certain relative autonomy and could have acted differently. The future, though it is not entirely open, is not entirely closed either (and, indeed, the degree of its openness is itself structurally determined).[26] In short, within a system characterized by total structural determinism, there would be no place for power.

Of course, one always has the alternative of stipulatively redefining 'power' in terms of structural determination. This is the path which Poulantzas took in his book *Political Power and Social Classes* (1973 [1968]). He defined his concept of power as '*the capacity of a social class to realize its specific objective interests*' (p. 104) and argued that this concept '*points to the effects of the structure on the relations of conflict between the practices of the various classes in "struggle"*'. In other words, power is not located in the levels of structures, but is an effect of the ensemble of these levels ...' (p. 99). Class relations are '*at every level relations of power*: power, however, is only a concept indicating the effect of the ensemble of the structures on *the relations of the practices of the various classes in conflict*' (p. 101). But this conceptual assimilation of power to structural determination simply serves to obscure a crucial distinction which it is theoretically necessary to make, and which the vocabulary of power articulates. My claim, in other words, is that to identify a given process as an 'exercise of power', rather than as a case of structural determination, is to assume that it is *in the exerciser's or exercisers' power* to act differently. In the case of a collective exercise of power, or the part of a group, or institution, etc., this is to imply that the members of the group or institution could have combined or organized to act differently.

The justification of this claim, and the key to the latter two difficulties involved in the identification of the process of exercising power, lies in the relation between power and responsibility.[27] The reason why identifying such an exercise involves the assumption that the exerciser(s) could have acted differently – and, where they are unaware of the consequences of their action or inaction, that they could have ascertained these – is that an attribution of power is at the same time an attribution of (partial or total) responsibility for certain consequences. The point, in other words, of locating power is to fix responsibility for consequences held to flow from the action, or inaction, of certain specifiable agents. We cannot here enter into a discussion of the notion of responsibility (and the problems of identifying collective responsibility): it is no less problematic – and essentially contested – a notion than the others examined in this essay. Nor can we here discuss the underlying theoretical (and non-empirical?) issue of how one determines where structural determination ends and power and responsibility begins. But it is worth noting, in conclusion, that C. Wright Mills perceived the relations I have argued for between these concepts in his distinction between *fate* and power. His 'sociological conception of fate' had, he wrote, 'to do with events in history that are beyond the control of any circle or groups of men (1) compact enough to be identifiable, (2) powerful enough to decide with consequence, and (3) in a position to foresee the consequences and so to be held accountable for historical events' (Mills 1959: 21). He argued in favour of attributing power to those in strategic positions who are able to initiate changes that are in the interests of broad segments of society but do not, claiming it to be 'now sociologically realistic, morally fair, and politically imperative to make demands upon men of power and to hold them responsible for specific courses of events' (p. 100).

9 Conclusion

The one-dimensional view of power offers a clear-cut paradigm for the behavioural study of decision-making power by political actors, but it inevitably takes over the bias of the political system under observation and is blind to the ways in which its political agenda is controlled. The two-dimensional view points the way to examining that bias and control, but conceives of them too narrowly: in a word, it lacks a sociological perspective within which to examine, not only decision-making and nondecision-making power, but also the various ways of suppressing latent conflicts within society. Such an examination poses a number of serious difficulties.

These difficulties are serious but not overwhelming. They certainly do not require us to consign the three-dimensional view of power to the realm of the merely metaphysical or the merely ideological. My conclusion, in short, is that a deeper analysis of power relations is possible – an analysis that is at once value-laden, theoretical and empirical.[28] A pessimistic attitude towards the possibility of such an analysis is unjustified. As Frey has written (1971: 1095), such pessimism amounts to saying: 'Why let things be difficult when, with just a little more effort, we can make them seem impossible?'

2

POWER, FREEDOM AND REASON

In this chapter I seek to broaden the discussion of the concept of power. I begin from the fact of unending disagreement about how power is to be conceived and ask whether we need the concept at all and, if so, what for. I will then draw a sort of conceptual map in order to situate and focus upon the argument of *PRV* and the debate of which it was part. Because *PRV* was a response and contribution to an ongoing debate within American political science, it was also caught up in the presuppositions of that debate whose shared concept of power, based on Dahl's 'intuitive idea' that '*A* has power over *B* to the extent that he can get *B* to do something that *B* would not otherwise do' (Dahl 1957 in Scott (ed.) 1994: vol. 2, p. 290), has been condemned as 'sterile' (Taylor 1984: 171). That condemnation was made in the light of subsequent theorizing about power, notably by Michel Foucault, whose treatment of power promised to broaden and deepen the discussion. I think the condemnation of the earlier debate is too dismissive: Dahl and his followers brought welcome and healthy precision, clarity and methodological rigour to the study of an admittedly narrow range of important questions. The contention of their critics was that their method was too restrictive, leading them to biased and complacent conclusions and preventing them from addressing wider questions concerning less overt and visible ways of securing the compliance of more or less willing subjects. By contrast, Foucault beamed floods of light on these questions, in an excessively rhetorical style entirely free of methodological rigour, but in a way that has stimulated much thinking and research in a variety of fields. As we shall see, Foucault's rhetoric has encouraged many to conceive of power in ways that suggest excitingly subversive implications for how we should think about freedom and rationality. However, that is not a path, I shall argue, down which we should travel.

Disagreements over 'Power'

We speak and write about power, in innumerable situations, and we usually know, or think we know, perfectly well what we mean. In daily life and in scholarly works, we discuss its location and its extent, who has more and who less, how to gain, resist, seize, harness, secure, tame, share, spread, distribute, equalize or maximize it, how to render it more effective and how to limit or avoid its effects. And yet, among those who have reflected on the matter, there is no agreement about to how to define it, how to conceive it, how to study it and, if it can be measured, how to measure it. There are endless debates about such questions, which show no sign of imminent resolution, and there is not even agreement about whether all this disagreement matters.

Different explanations have been advanced for why this is so. One suggestion is that the *word* 'power' is polysemic: like, say, the words 'social' and 'political', it has multiple and diverse meanings, appropriate to different settings and concerns. Another is that, like the word 'game', 'power' denotes a range of different objects or referents that have no single common essence, no one property that they all share other than their name: it exhibits what Wittgenstein called 'family resemblance'. A third, related suggestion, also following Wittgenstein, is that different concepts of power have their place in different local 'language games' and that this entails that the search for a single concept of power is illusory. A fourth suggestion is that power is an 'essentially contested concept'. This is to say that there is indeed a single concept of power but that it is one of those concepts that 'essentially involve endless disputes about their proper uses on the part of their users' (Gallie 1955–6: 123).

There is something to be said for all four explanations. Plainly, we use the vocabulary of power in countless different ways in different contexts and for different purposes. Hobbes wrote of mankind's 'perpetual and restless desire of power after power, that ceaseth only in death' (Hobbes 1946[1651]: 64) whereas Burke wrote that 'liberty, when men act in bodies, is *power*' (Burke 1910[1790]: 7). It is not self-evident what talk of horse power and nuclear power, of the power of grace and the power of punishment, of power struggles and the power of a group to 'act in concert', of the balance of power and the separation of powers, of the 'power of the powerless' and the corruptions of absolute power all have in common. Moreover, different ways of conceiving power are natural to differing perspectives and purposes. Edward Said asks: 'why imagine power in the first place, and what is the relationship between one's motive for imagining power and the image one ends up with?' (Said 1986: 151). His suggestion is that the latter largely derives from the former. So, as Peter Morriss observes, in using the notion of power, the 'CIA don't want to know the sorts of things about a society that a fervent democrat, worried about the society's practices, does' and 'the utilitarian celebrating the amount of power to satisfy wants is not disagreeing with the romantic bemoaning the lack of power for self-development' (Morriss 2002: 205).

And yet there are disagreements about where power lies, how far it extends and how its effects are brought about which it is plausible to see, not as disputes over the facts but over how we should characterize them, as contests about how we should think of power: about how power is to be conceptualized. For, as I shall argue, how we think of power is controversial and can have significant consequences. When we try to understand power, how we think about it relates in a number of ways to what we are trying to understand. Our aim is to represent it in a way that is suited for description and explanation. But our conception of it may result from and be shaped by what we are trying to describe and explain. It may also affect and shape it: how we think of power may serve to reproduce and reinforce power structures and relations, or alternatively it may challenge and subvert them. It may contribute to their continued functioning, or it may unmask their principles of operation, whose effectiveness is increased by their being hidden from view. To the extent that this is so, conceptual and methodological questions are inescapably political and so what 'power' means is 'essentially contested', in the sense that reasonable people, who disagree morally and politically, may agree about the facts but disagree about where power lies.

In the face of these disagreements, and the difficulties from which they spring, doubts are sometimes expressed about whether power is a suitable concept for purposes of *analysis*. Perhaps it is a 'lay' or 'folk' concept rather than a 'scientific' one, a 'category of practice' rather than a 'category of analysis'.[1] A general argument to this effect might be the following. Power (as I shall argue below) is a *dispositional* concept, comprising a conjunction of conditional or hypothetical statements specifying what would occur under a range of circumstances if and when the power is exercised. Thus power refers to an ability or capacity of an agent or agents, which they may or may not exercise. But how can that be explanatory? If the goal of social science is to reduce contingency and arrive at law-like explanations of outcomes that yield determinate predictions, then, obviously, specifying dispositions or abilities is going to be useless – as useless as Molière's doctor's attempt to explain the effects of opium by its *virtus dormitiva*, or 'dormitive power'.[2]

So Bruno Latour writes that 'power' is a 'pliable and empty term'. It names 'what has to be explained by the action of the others who obey': it 'may be used as a convenient way to *summarize* the consequences of a collective action' but 'it cannot also *explain* what holds the collective action in place'. And so,

Latour breezily suggests, 'the notion of power should be abandoned' (Latour 1986: 266, 265, 278). And in a widely noticed article James March argued that 'power is a disappointing concept', giving us 'surprisingly little purchase in reasonable models of complex systems of social choice' (March 1966: 70). In view of the difficulties to which I have alluded, he voiced doubts that power is 'real and meaningful' and that there 'must be some fire behind the smoke' (68). March suggested that we are tempted to think this because of the 'obviousness of power' but that we should resist the temptation. We 'can scarcely talk about our daily life or major social and political phenomena without talking about power' and we think, it seems mistakenly, that 'power is patently real' (68).

In *PRV* I take exactly the contrary position. There I suggest that power is real and effective in a remarkable variety of ways, some of them indirect and some hidden, and that, indeed, it is at its most effective when least accessible to observation, to actors and observers alike, thereby presenting empirically minded social scientists with a neat paradox. In suggesting this, I do not mean to imply that they should therefore give up. On the contrary, they have three lines of action: (1) to search for observable mechanisms of what I call power's third dimension, (2) to find ways of falsifying it, and (3) to identify relations, characteristics and phenomena of power for which the first and second dimensions cannot account. Of course, even if such attempts to identify it in empirically falsifiable terms fail, that does not mean that the phenomena do not exist, only that we lack the methodological tools and skills for doing so.

As will become clear, *PRV* offers a very partial and one-sided account of the topic. For one thing, it focuses entirely on the *exercise* of power and, for another, it deals only with asymmetric power – the power of some *over* others – and, moreover, with only a sub-type of this, namely, the securing of compliance to domination. Furthermore, it treats only of binary relations between actors who are assumed to have unitary interests. Plainly a fuller account must obviously relax these simplifying assumptions and address power among multiple actors with divergent interests. Even within a binary relationship, such as a marriage, after all, domination may characterize only some of the interactions between the parties; in either direction, and on some issues their interests may not conflict.[3] As we shall see, a better definition of power in social life than that offered in *PRV* is in terms of agents' abilities to bring about significant effects, specifically by furthering their own interests and/or affecting the interests of others, whether positively or negatively. So I now ask a further question: Why do we need this concept? What do we need the concept of power for?

It is odd that, despite all that has been written about power, I have only been able to find one author who has addressed this question, namely Peter Morriss, in his book *Power: A Philosophical Analysis* (Morriss 2002), and I shall build on his discussion here. He argues that there are three contexts in which we talk of power, which he calls 'practical', 'moral' and 'evaluative'.

First, the **practical** context. Citing Brian Barry's observation that the powerful people in any society must include those whom the CIA would want to bribe (Barry 1974: 189), he observes that you need to know the powers of others 'to get them to do things *for* you, or you may want to make sure that you don't run the risk of them doing unwelcome things *to* you' (Morriss 2002: 37). We need to know our own powers and those of others in order to find our way around a world populated by human agents, individual and collective, of whose powers we need to be apprised if we are to have a chance of surviving and flourishing. And of course our own powers will in part depend on harnessing and evading or diminishing the powers of others. We carry around in our heads maps of such agents' powers – of their dispositional abilities to affect our interests – usually as tacit knowledge, which allows us some measure of prediction and control. Power functions here (as Latour suggests) as a way of summarizing much-needed counterfactual knowledge of what agents would do under hypothetical conditions. But note that this knowledge operates at various levels. We need to know what the formal powers of officials are. But we also need to know what they can really do for or to us, if they choose, given what we know of their situation and character. And we may also need to know what they might do for or to us in unexpected circumstances, or if under pressure or behaving irrationally. Thomas Hobbes thought that man seeks power to assure 'the way of his future desires' and, even in a world less ruthlessly competitive and threatening than the one he pictured, such assurance requires knowledge of the powers of others.

Second, the **moral** context. Here the key idea is that of *responsibility*. According to Terence Ball,

> when we say that someone has power or is powerful we are ... *assigning responsibility* to a human agent or agency for bringing (or failing to bring) about certain outcomes that impinge upon the interests of other human beings. (Ball 1976: 249)

Citing this, Morriss argues that the connection between power and responsibility is 'essentially negative: you can deny all responsibility by demonstrating lack of power' (Morriss 2002: 39). Thus an alibi for a crime consists in showing that you could not have done it; and an excuse for failing to prevent lamentable events sometimes (but not always) consists in showing that you could not have prevented them. But here, I think, Morriss does not go far enough. He is, of course, right to say that when 'it comes to holding people morally responsible – praising and blaming them – it is invariably their actions (and omissions) that we look at, not their powers' (21–2). But in deciding where power in society lies – that is, who the more powerful actors are, and which are more and which less powerful – we have to make decisions as to where, among all the influences at work, to focus our attention. The powerful are those whom we judge or can hold to be responsible for significant outcomes. That is why I quoted C. Wright Mills's idea that we should attribute power to those in strategic positions who are able to initiate changes that are in the interests of broad segments of society but do not, and his claim that it is 'now sociologically realistic, morally fair and politically imperative to make demands upon the men of power and to hold them responsible for specific courses of action' (Mills 1959: 100). This, incidentally, shows that the question of responsibility is not only 'moral' but also, and mainly, political.

To illustrate the foregoing, consider the following example.[4] Because of the way the housing market functions in large cities, many ordinary non-affluent people lack access to decent, afford-able housing. This can be seen as a *structural* problem insofar as it is the uncoordinated and unintended outcome of the independent actions of large numbers of actors pursuing their varied respective interests – renters, home-buyers, mortgage lenders, real-estate brokers, developers, land-use regulators, transport planners, and so on. But insofar as individuals or groups lack access because of the actions or inactions of other identifiable individuals or groups, who by acting otherwise could make a difference, then it makes sense to see the latter as powerful *because responsible*. So, of course, at the individual level, discriminatory landlords and corrupt officials have power; but, at the city, cor-porate or national levels, politicians and others in 'strategic posi-tions', who individually or in alliance could make a difference, can be viewed as powerful to the extent that they *fail* to address remediable problems.

Third, the **evaluative** context. Here what is at issue is the judging, or evaluation, of social systems, of 'the distribution – and extent – of power within a society'. Morriss distinguishes 'two broad perspectives' with respect to this issue: we may be concerned about 'the extent to which citizens have the power to meet their own needs and wants' or else about the extent to which societies 'give their citizens freedom from the power of others'. The first indicates impotence, or the lack of power, the second domination, or being subject to the power of another or others, and 'these are not the same and need not be found together'. Indeed, it is an error to assume that 'what is wrong if you are powerless is that you are in someone else's power, and that that someone else must be responsible for your powerless-ness if you are to have a valid complaint'. From this Morriss con-cludes that 'if people are powerless because they live in a certain sort of society – that is, they would have had more power if the

social arrangements were changed – then that, itself, is a condemnation of that society. A radical critique of a society requires
us to evaluate *that* society, not distribute praise or blame to
people' (pp. 40–2).

Morriss is right to warn against what we might call 'the para-
noid fallacy' of *assuming* that powerlessness results from domination – that when people lack power, it can only be because of the
machinations of the powerful.[5] But his suggestion that, in our
actual world, these are sharply separate questions – that 'when
we censure *a set of social arrangements*, all that needs to be shown is
that it, rather than the sufferers themselves, is responsible for the
sufferings that people have within that society. One does not need
to establish that the harm is intended or foreseen by anybody'
(p. 41) – does not withstand scrutiny. For one thing, people are
often rendered and kept powerless by the deliberate activities
of others – such as the discriminating landlords and corrupt
officials mentioned above. But, in any case, as I shall argue in
the pages that follow, power should not be conceived narrowly
as requiring intention, actual foresight and positive actions (as
opposed to failing to act): the power of the powerful consists in
their being capable of and responsible for affecting (negatively
or positively) the (subjective and/or objective) interests of
others. On this broader view of power, the issues of powerlessness
and of domination will no longer seem so obviously separate and
locked into distinct perspectives. (Indeed, if we think of powerlessness as an *injustice,* rather than as bad luck or misfortune, is
that not because we believe that there are those in a position
to reduce or remedy it?) As suggested in the discussion above
of responsibility, the powerful will include those who both contribute to and are in a position to reduce or remedy others'
powerlessness. Where this is not feasible, we encounter structural limits to power. Here, of course, there looms up the large,
and largely opaque, topic of the relations between power and
structure and the case for seeing power as tied to agency, about
which I have written elsewhere (Lukes 1977a; for contrasting
views see Layder 1985 and Hayward 2000). Let it here suffice
to repeat only one thought: that social life can only properly be

understood as an interplay of power and structure, a web of possibilities for agents, whose nature is both active and structured, to make choices and pursue strategies within given limits, which in consequence expand and contract over time.[6]

The Concept of Power

It seems that there are several, even many concepts of power. But when and how are we to distinguish these concepts one from another? And in the case of a dispute about where power lies or about its extent or effects, how can we tell whether the disputants are disagreeing about the facts, applying different concepts or engaging in a contest over the same concept? And does it matter? In what follows I shall maintain that it does matter. I shall propose that there is, indeed, a single, comprehensive, extremely general or generic concept of power common to all cases and that, in application to human agents (individual and collective) it exhibits two distinct variants (which we can provisionally, but misleadingly, label as the concepts of 'power to' and 'power over'), where the latter is a subspecies of the former, and that alternative ways of conceiving a version of the latter exhibit what has been called 'essential contestedness', with significant consequences for our understanding of social life.

John Locke sought to capture the generic sense of 'power' when he defined having it as being 'able to make, or able to receive, any change' (Locke 1975[1690]: 111). Even that, however, is not general enough, for it excludes the power to resist change in the face of a changing environment. So let us say, extending Locke's definition, that having power is being able to make or to receive any change, or to resist it. Though extremely general, this has several specific implications. It implies that power is a dispositional concept. It identifies a capacity: power is a potentiality, not an actuality – indeed a potentiality that may never be actualized. As Anthony Kenny observes, failure to see this has frequently led to two different forms of reductionism, often combined and often confused, depending on whether the attempt was to reduce a power to its exercise or to its vehicle. Hume when he said that the distinction between a power and its exercise was wholly frivolous wanted to reduce powers to their exercises. Descartes when he attempted to identify all the powers of bodies with their geometrical properties wanted to reduce powers to their vehicles.   (Kenny 1975: 10)

Among present-day social scientists the 'exercise fallacy' has been committed by those for whom power can only mean the causing of an observable sequence of events. This has led behavioural political scientists (such as Dahl, Polsby and others), for example, to equate power with success in decision-making. To be powerful is to win: to prevail over others in conflict situations. But, as we have seen, such victories can be very misleading as to where power really lies. Raymond Aron was rightly critical of 'the kind of sociology that prides itself on being strictly empirical and operational' and that 'questions the utility of the term "power" to the extent that it designates a potential that is never made manifest except through acts (decisions)' (Aron 1964 in Lukes (ed.) 1986: 256). The 'vehicle fallacy' is committed by those tempted by the idea that power must mean whatever goes into operation when power is activated. This idea has led sociologists and military analysts, for example, to equate power with power resources, such as wealth and status, or military forces and weapons.[7] But having the means of power is not the same as being powerful. As the United States discovered in Vietnam and postwar Iraq, having military superiority is not the same as having power. In short, observing the exercise of power can give evidence of its possession, and counting power resources can be a clue to its distribution, but power is a capacity, and not the exercise or the vehicle of that capacity.

These points are elementary but failure to grasp them has led many distinguished minds astray. Thinking clearly about power is not easy and it gets more difficult, offering more opportunities for confusion when we try to think about power in social life, not least because we all talk and write about it all the time and in confusingly different ways. What I seek to do in this chapter is to draw a sort of conceptual map of a landscape with figures – the figures being those who have taken distinctive positions in the debates about power. The point of such a map is to present to the reader an ordered way of conceptualizing power that stays as close as possible to our everyday uses of the vocabulary of power and related terms, while attempting to delineate a coherent conceptual structure that makes clear what questions about power arise, how they relate to one another and why disagreements about how to answer them persist, and why they matter. This will involve decisions at various points, where there are alternative and conflicting current linguistic usages, to accept some and reject others.

When the generic sense of 'power' is used in relation to social life, it refers to the capacities of social agents. Let us agree that these agents may be individuals or collectivities, of various kinds. To begin with individuals, we can, I hope, further agree, along with Aristotle, that, unlike natural powers, such as the power of fire to burn wood, there are human powers that are typically 'two-way powers, powers which can be exercised at will'; for, as Kenny remarks, 'a rational agent, presented with all the necessary external conditions for exercising a power, may choose not to do so' (Kenny 1975: 53). But, Kenny further observes, there are also human powers that are not two-way, or subject to choice, as when if 'someone speaks a language I know in my hearing it isn't in my power not to understand it' (ibid.) Such 'passive' powers, where the agent 'receives' rather than 'makes' changes, experiencing rather than bringing about the outcome, can be of great significance: compare the passive power of the starving to recuperate by being nourished, with the active power of the religious ascetic to starve. So we may say that human powers are, typically, abilities activated by agents choosing to do so (though the choice may be highly constrained, and alternative paths unlikely to be taken) and also passive powers which the agents may possess irrespective of their wills.

Moreover, the agents may be individual or collective agents. The latter can be of many kinds: states, institutions, associations, alliances, social movements, groups, clubs and so on. Collectivities typically have co-ordination problems but, where these do not exist or can be overcome, so that the collectivity can act, then it too can be said to have power and that power may also be two-way: it may or may not be activated. A corollary of these points is that in what follows we will not attribute power to structures or relations or processes that cannot be characterized as agents.

The attribution of specific powers to particular agents, individual or collective, can be relatively straightforward. The question 'Does a certain agent have the power to bring about such and such an outcome' is clear-cut, though the answer (in advance of a successful exercise of the power in question) is fallible, depending on an (indeterminate) range of conjectures about counterfactuals — scenarios in which some factors are held constant and others varied. The really tricky problems arise when we seek, as we invariably do, to aggregate and compare powers. We very commonly ask questions such as: Has the President's power increased? Is trade union power in decline? What are the dangers and limits of power of the world's only superpower? Who is the most powerful member of the team? How can the excluded and the marginalized be empowered? Such questions involve assessments of the extent of agents' power overall, comparisons of its varying extent across time (comparing present overall power with the past or the projected future) and comparisons of the overall power of different agents.

To arrive at an assessment of an agent's overall power involves, as we shall see, two kinds of judgment about what is relevant to the assessment: judgments about the scope of the concept of power one is using (roughly, how wide the lens is through which one is looking for power) and judgments about the significance of the outcomes the agents are capable of bringing about. For, in the first place, the wider the scope of what, in the view of one's conceptual framework, is going to count as power, the more power in the world one will be able to see. And, secondly, not all outcomes will have equal weight in assessing the extent of an agent's power. Different outcomes have differential impact on the interests of the various parties concerned (including the agent's own): many of my powers are trivial (such as my capacity to move currents of air about when I speak), while a judge who can impose a death sentence has greater power than one who cannot. In assessing overall power, value judgments will always be necessary to determine which outcomes count for more and which for less.

But social power, as we have so far considered it, whether held individually or collectively, does not yet correspond to what, in common parlance and in the writings of philosophers, historians and social scientists, 'power' is commonly taken to identify. In this more restrictive but widespread understanding, 'power' is explicitly[8] relational and asymmetrical: to have power is to have power *over* another or others. The distinction between the general sense of a social actor's power to effect or receive outcomes and this more restricted sense has nowhere been better captured than by Spinoza, in the Latin language, when, in his *Tractatus Politicus* he distinguishes between '*potentia*' and '*potestas*'. '*Potentia*' signifies the power of things in nature, including persons, 'to exist and act'). '*Potestas*' is used when speaking of being *in the power of* another. According to Spinoza,

> one individual is subject to the right of another, or dependent upon him, for as long as he is subject to the other's power; and possessed of his own right, or free, in so far as he can repel all force, take what vengeance he pleases for harm done to him, and, to speak generally, live as his own nature and judgment dictate.   (Spinoza 1958[1677]: 273)

The Latin words, as expounded by Spinoza, perfectly capture this conceptual distinction on which the rest of this chapter draws. They do so more precisely than the available terms in various live languages. In German, it is partially caught by the distinction between '*Macht*', on the one hand, and '*Herrschaft*', on the other. In English, however, 'power' straddles it, as does '*potere* in Italian (though '*potenza*' is equivalent to '*potentia*', whereas '*potestà*' is much narrower than '*potestas*'). Both '*pouvoir*' and '*puissance*' in French cover both senses, though only the latter normally signifies power in its proper sense as capacity, while the former tends to denote its exercise (Aron 1964) – thereby generating confusion when '*pouvoir*' is translated as 'power'. In Russian, according to Ledyaev, the word '*vlast*', normally translated as 'power', seems to mean *potestas*, since it 'is usually used for the description of someone's ability to control (dominate, compel, influence) *others*: "power" is imagined as something that is "over" us, that limits our freedom, creates obstacles, etc.' (Ledyaev 1997: 95).

The concept of asymmetric power, or power as *potestas*, or 'power over', is, therefore, a sub-concept or version of the concept of power as *potentia*: it is the ability to have another or others *in your power*, by constraining their choices, thereby securing their compliance. Such power is the ability to effect a distinctive range of outcomes: among them those captured by the concept of *domination*, and such closely related notions as subordination, subjugation, control, conformism, acquiescence and docility. But now a whole new set of questions arises. How is power as domination – and in particular how are the outcomes indicated and the mechanisms that bring them about – to be understood, theorized about and studied empirically? This is the subject-matter of much literature and recent debates, including the so-called 'power debate' to which *PRV* was a contribution.

A Conceptual Map

Having sketched the broad outlines of the concept of power, I now turn to delineating a more detailed conceptual map. Let us begin with the wider notion of power as *potentia*.

Consider first what we may call the *issue-scope* of power. This I shall take to refer to the number of different issues over which I can determine the outcome. Suppose that you and I are both

ministers in some government. I may be able to push through a
policy to which I am fully committed but be unable to win on any
other issue, whereas you may be capable of winning on several
different issues. Of course, individuating 'issues' may be controversial and, obviously, the significance of the issues on which you
can prevail will be pertinent in assessing your power (see below),
but (other things being equal), the wider the scope within which
one can bring about significant outcomes, the more power one
has. Single-issue power can be extremely important (consider
the power of pressure groups, such as Greenpeace) but broaden-
ing the scope means (again, other things being equal) increasing
the ability to bring about significant outcomes. This distinction bears on an analogy sometimes drawn between power
and money (see Parsons 1963). To have single-issue power is to
lack liquidity – what you can buy with it is highly restricted –
whereas multi-issue power is fungible and can be spent in several
alternative ways.

Second, consider what we may call the *contextual range* of
power. In which circumstances is it assumed to be operative?
Does 'power' identify what an agent can bring about only
under the conditions that actually obtain or under various alternative conditions? If the first, you are powerful if you can produce the appropriate outcomes only if present circumstances
enable you to do so (for example, a particular configuration of
given voting preferences enables your vote to decide the outcome); if the second, you can do it in a range of possible circumstances. The first identifies what one is able to do in a specific
place and time, given the conditions that obtain there and then;
the second the ability that one can deploy across a range of (standard) contexts. Peter Morriss calls the first 'ableness' and the
second 'ability', though I shall not follow that rather artificial
usage here.[9] I shall call the first 'context-bound' and the second
'context-transcending' ability. The distinction throws an interesting light on the relation between power and resistance –
and, more generally, between power and obstacles of all kinds.[10]
For my context-bound ability here and now is maximized if the
resistance or obstacles to my power are minimized, whereas my

context-transcending ability is the greater, the greater is the resistance or the number and magnitude of the obstacles I can (given my existing capacities and resources) overcome.

Third, consider the relation between power and *intention*. Bertrand Russell defined power as 'the production of intended effects' (Russell 1938: 25), Max Weber and C. Wright Mills connect power with the realization of the 'will' of the powerful, and many, like Goldman, think that power involves 'getting what one wants' (Goldman 1972, 1974a, b). Obviously, some abilities are abilities to bring about intended consequences. (There are actually two possibilities here: the ability to bring about what I actually intend, and the ability to bring about what I might, hypothetically, intend). If I possess such an ability, I can, given the appropriate resources, under favourable circumstances, bring it about (if I can bring it about only in *these* circumstances, it is context-bound) and, if I have such an ability, you can normally count on me to bring about the desired result, if I so choose. Yet most of our actions bring in their wake innumerable chains of unintended consequences, some of them highly significant, and some of these seem obvious instances of power. Powerful people, for example, induce deferential behaviour in others but may not intend to. Pollsters can unintentionally influence the outcomes of elections. Routine rule following can have unanticipated consequences as the environment changes. And, indeed, as argued in Chapter 1, unintended consequences of power can be unforeseen (though to count as power they must be foreseeable). The field of economic power abounds in such instances, where decisions – to raise prices, say, or to invest – foreclose or enable opportunities and choices for unknown others, and creditors have power over debtors. What actors intentionally do always generates chains of unintended consequences and it is implausible to deny that some of these manifest their power. Of course, those which frustrate their intentions may signify a lack of power to control events, but, as argued earlier, we can properly hold responsible, or accountable, those who have the power to advance or harm others' interests but fail to realize or attend to this.

Fourth, consider the distinction between *active* and *inactive* power. To *exercise* power is to perform actions. Indeed the very phrase 'exercising power' suggests such activity, while the phrase 'exerting power' suggests even more strenuous activity. There are three points to be made here. First, the distinction can be merely verbal: a vote is a failure to abstain; an abstention is a failure to vote. But second, and more deeply, 'negative' actions, or failures to act, can sometimes properly be seen as actions with consequences (indeed they can only be specified in terms of their consequences). Sometimes, therefore, abstention or non-intervention can be a form of power, as with US Steel in Gary, Indiana. Whether we count an absence of action as an action depends on a judgment as to whether such action has significant causal consequences and on whether we are disposed to regard the actor who fails to act as responsible, in one or another sense, for so failing. But this is precisely what is at issue in deciding the question of whether negative actions can instantiate power. There is no good reason for excluding failures positively to act from the scope of power on principle. Of course, there must be some criterion for selecting the relevant non-events as actions, or failures positively to 'intervene': a baseline of expectation against which, counterfactually, the putative intervention in question can be seen as both feasible and one for which the agent could be held responsible. Of course, the power exemplified by not acting thus implies the ability to act (and vice versa). But in the analysis of power, therefore, positive actions have no special significance. To act can be a sign of weakness (for instance, conforming to the demands of repressive regimes – such as voting in a Communist election in Soviet times) and the index of an actor's power can be his ability to avoid or resist performing positive actions. So the US under the Bush administration shows its power by not ratifying the Kyoto protocols on climate change and by not participating in the International Criminal Court.

Moreover, the features of agents that make them powerful include those that render activity unnecessary. If I can achieve the appropriate outcomes without having to act, because of the

attitudes of others towards me or because of a favourable align-
ment of social relations and forces facilitating such outcomes,
then my power is surely all the greater. It may derive from
what has been called the rule of anticipated reactions (Friedrich
1941: 589–91), where others anticipate my expected reactions to
unwelcome activity (or inactivity) on their part, thereby aiming
to forestall overt coercion: a clear example is the self-censorship
practised by writers and journalists under authoritarian
regimes. The inactive power accumulated by such regimes is, of
course, often the residue of past uses of active power, often coercive and sometimes on a massive scale. But not all inactive power
results from previous active power in this direct way. Sometimes,
indeed, the anticipated reactions can be misanticipated reactions: that is, mistaken because deriving from misplaced fears.
Moreover, inactive power can derive from powerful agents'
properties rather than from their actions, as with the power of
attraction. Charismatic power, like magnetism, exemplifies this
(though in reality charismatic leaders usually work hard and
with skill to achieve their effects), and the inactive power that
derives from status, inducing deference, relieves those who are
secure in their positions from the need to focus on acting to preserve them. So James Scott suggests that 'the impact of power is
most readily observed in acts of deference, subordination and
ingratiation' and comments that power means 'not *having* to act
or, more precisely, the capacity to be more negligent and casual
about any single performance' (Scott 1990: 28–9). The distinction between active and inactive power can be thought of in
terms of the relation between power and costs (see Goldman
1974b). If my power declines as the costs of exercising it increase,
and if having actively to exercise power is itself regarded as such
a cost, then one can say that inactive power reduces this cost
towards zero.

Figure 1 illustrates the foregoing discussion. The four columns
represent the four aspects just considered, presented as disjunc-
tions (though they are all in fact continua): each item in the top
row represents one alternative, each item in the bottom row its
negation. The power of a social agent that is described in the top

Issue scope	Contextual range	Intentionality	Activity
Single-issue	Context-bound	Intended consequences	Active exercise
Multi-issue	Context-transcending	Unintended consequences	Inactive enjoyment

Figure 1

row is (other things being equal) augmented further if it successively occupies each box in the second row. Suppose I am able to prevail on a particular issue in these circumstances, achieving what I intend and exercising my will. Is my power not increased to the extent that I can do so over a variety of issues, in a range of different circumstances, generating significant unintended consequences and without having to lift a finger?

What we have so far seen is that the ability that 'power' names can have a variable extension, depending on its issue-scope, its contextual range, and the degree of non-intentionality and inactivity its manifestation involves. But notice that all these bases for variation apply to instances of power taken severally, or one by one: the power of any given agent is greater if any of these is increased in respect of that agent. But we do not only attribute power to agents, identifying what power they have and estimating how much they have; we also make comparative judgments of power. We want to know how much more power one has than another. In some cases their power may have the same issue-scope. With respect to an agent's power over a given issue, or a given set of issues, we can say that another agent's power, over that issue or set of issues, is greater if it exhibits greater contextual range, brings about further significant consequences or involves less cost to the agent. In other cases, one agent's issue-scope may include that of another. If your scope is greater than mine (that is, you can bring about all the outcomes I can and more), we can say that your power exceeds mine. But, of course, most power comparisons are more complex than either of these

cases, for, most commonly, we are comparing the power of different agents over different issues. We are interested in comparing
their overall power in cases where the scope of their respective
power is non-coincident and often non-overlapping.

Such comparisons bring out a further aspect in which the
shape or extension of power can vary. For I will have more
(overall) power than you if I can bring about outcomes that are
more 'significant' than those you can bring about. But how do
we judge the significance of outcomes? The most natural
answer is: we look at their effects upon the *interests* of the agents
involved. The concept of 'interests' points us towards what is
important in people's lives. As we shall see, this can be interpreted purely 'subjectively', so that what is in my interests is
decided by what is important to me; or else it can be interpreted
in a way that incorporates 'objective' judgments, concerning
what benefits and harms me, where what counts as benefit and
harm is not decided by my preferences or judgments. In comparing the power of agents across different scopes, or sets of issues,
we unavoidably introduce judgments about the extent to which
and ways in which their power furthers their own interests
and affects the interests of others. Normally, we assume that the
power of the powerful furthers their interests (though Susan
Strange has an interesting discussion of the ways in which the
US's financial power can ricochet back on its possessors to
their ultimate disadvantage – see Strange 1990). Aside from
that assumption, it is the impact of power on others' interests
that provides the basis for judgment concerning its extent.

Thus, as already suggested, most would be inclined to say
that a judge with the power of sentencing to life or death has
greater power than a judge without that power: the second
judge might have a wider range of lesser sentences but the first
would have greater power. Similarly, the Mafia, where it holds
sway, has greater power than other influential groups, organizations and governmental agencies, in part by virtue of the greater
harms it can inflict and the greater benefits it can bestow. The
power of multi-media magnates is greater than that of, say,
advertisers or rock stars. If I can affect your central or basic

interests, my power (in relation to you) is greater than someone who affects you only superficially. But, of course, the question of where people's interests lie, of what is basic or central to their lives and what is superficial, is inherently controversial. Any answer to it must involve taking sides in current moral, political and, indeed, philosophical, controversies. It follows that, for this reason, comparisons of power, involving such assessment of its impact on agents' interests, can never avoid value judgments.

There are alternative ways of conceiving of agents' interests. One way is the purely subjective way of straightforwardly identifying them with *preferences* (as opposed to passing wants or whims).[11] Such preferences may, as economists say, be 'revealed', as in market behaviour or in voting behaviour in actual choice situations. I call such preferences *overt*. Alternatively, they may be more or less hidden from view, because unrevealed in actual choice situations: they may take the form of half-articulated or unarticulated grievances or aspirations which, because of the bias of the dominant political agenda or the prevailing culture, are not heard and may not even be voiced. I call such preferences *covert*. Behind the equation of interests with preferences, overt or covert, lies the Benthamite view that everyone is the best judge of his or her own interests: to discover where people's interests lie, either you observe their choice behaviour or else you infer, from a close observation of what they say and do, what they would choose were choices available that are currently unavailable.

An alternative way of conceiving interests is to see them as the necessary conditions of human *welfare*: what individuals generally need in order to live lives that are satisfactory by their own lights, whatever those lights may be. Here I have in mind what political philosophers variously call 'primary goods' (Rawls) or 'resources' (Dworkin) that satisfy 'basic needs' (of which there various alternative accounts) or else endow people with 'basic human capabilities' (Sen) or 'central capabilities' (Nussbaum). These are all various ways of specifying conditions that enable people to pursue their various purposes and conceptions of what makes life valuable, and without which that pursuit is frustrated or severely impeded. Among such welfare interests are such basic items as health, adequate nourishment, bodily integrity, shelter, personal security, an unpolluted environment, and so on. Some, notably John Rawls, point to 'rights and liberties, opportunities and powers, income and wealth' (Rawls 1972: 92), and thereby raise the question of cultural specificity. Which of these welfare interests can be treated as universal human interests and neutral between ways of life, and which are internal to particular regions of culture (see Nussbaum 2000: 34–110)? But, whatever the final answer to this question, welfare interests, thus conceived, are not preference-dependent, and so they can be thought of as objective. Their status as interests of persons does not derive from their being desired by them; conditions that damage your health are against your interests, in this sense, whatever your preferences, and even if you actively seek to promote them.

A third way of conceiving interests is to see them neither as preferences nor as the necessary conditions of leading any worthwhile life, but rather as constitutive of *well-being*: that is, comprising the leading of such a life itself. Thus your interests may be manifest in the focal aims or long-term goals in terms of which you seek to shape your life, or in the 'meta-preferences' or 'strong evaluations' in terms of which you judge which desires and preferences would make your life go better (see Taylor 1985: vol. 1: 15–44; vol. 2: 230–47), or in the whole network of desires, preferences and meta-preferences that living such a life involves, which you may or may not endorse (see Feinberg 1984). Here one's interests are given by the content of leading a worthwhile life. Of course, what counts as worthwhile or valuable and what counts as worthless or wasteful remains a deep, central and controversial ethical question – as does the question of how it is to be answered. All I mean to do here is to draw attention to the point that interests understood this way are also not straightforwardly preference-dependent, since this view of interests as wellbeing allows, indeed assumes, that people can in fact prefer to lead lives that are against what they may recognize to be their well-being.

So contestable judgments of significance partly determine one's assessment of an agent's overall power, and in a variety of ways. As Morriss observes, '[p]eople are the more powerful the more important the results they can obtain are' (Morriss 2002: 89). Furthermore, if I can affect others' interests more than you can, on some view of interests, then that (other things being equal) is grounds for supposing that my power is greater than yours. But, as we have seen, there are various views of interests. And how must I affect their interests? Favourably or unfavourably? Must I further them or harm them? Many writers on power just assume the latter:[12] that to have power is to act against others' interests. This assumption may well derive from a focus on the view of power as *potestas*, or power over others (to be considered below), though, as we shall see, this can also be interest-favouring. But there is really no reason for supposing that the powerful always threaten, rather than sometimes advance, the interests of others; sometimes, indeed, the use of power can benefit all, albeit usually unequally. And is my power the greater if I can *either* favour or disfavour your interests? And when seeking to assess an agent's overall power comparatively, how do we weigh the ability to favour others' interests with the ability to disfavour them? And how do numbers count? How many persons must I affect, in respect of their interests, to have more power? How do I compare affecting many persons' interests superficially with few persons' interests deeply? The truth is that the concept of power as such furnishes no decision rules for answering such questions. They can only be decided in the light of a set of conventions or a prior background theory or, indeed, on a case-by-case basis, in the light of contextual considerations.

Let us now turn to the more restricted notion of power as *potestas*, where an agent or agents have power over another or others. To have such power is to be able to constrain the choices they face, thereby securing their compliance. It is, therefore, the ability to secure that compliance, so that both constraint and compliance are necessary: the powerful agent may have the ability to

83

impose the constraint but has power only if, when the constraint is imposed, the subject complies. The compliance may be unwilling or it may be willing. In the former case, power is coercive. In the latter case, power requires the compliance of willing subjects.[13] But, as Amy Allen notices, such constraining power 'must be a broader concept than *domination*' (Allen 1999: 125), since, leaving masochists aside, we assume that domination works against the interests of the dominated, and yet such power and dependency (which is the state of being subject to it) may sometimes favour, or at least not disfavour, the interests of those who are subject to it.

Thomas Wartenberg's study (Wartenberg 1990), which focuses on the notion of 'power over', distinguishes between domination and such apparently beneficent power. One instance of such power is paternalism, as in legislation requiring the wearing of seat-belts, where A, seeking to avert harm or promote some benefit to B, may act against B's current wants or preferences, thereby limiting B's freedom to act. Wartenberg distinguishes this, in turn, from other forms of beneficent power which he labels 'transformative', citing feminist writings on mothering as examples of using power to empower another, by increasing the other's resources, capabilities, effectiveness and ability to act. He offers as further examples apprenticeship, teaching, parenting and therapy, citing Plato's account of a domineering Socrates in the *agora* creating fertile confusion in his young interlocutors so that they might achieve self-knowledge and self-determination. And to these one could add the obvious instances of power in command–obedience relationships that are indispensable to valued co-operative activities, as in armies, orchestra conducting and sports coaching. Richard Sennett has recently made a different case for seeing value in being subject to power, by questioning the widespread view that dependency, outside the sphere of intimate relations, always demeans, arguing that the 'liberal canon' takes for granted a 'concept of adulthood' according to which dependency is inherently shameful (Sennett 2003: 102). He is right about the liberal canon's rejection of dependency: Locke contrasted the 'subjection of a child to his parents' with the 'freedom of a man at years of discretion' which is 'grounded on his having reason' (Locke 1946[1690]: 31), Kant wrote of enlightenment as emergence from self-incurred immaturity by thinking for oneself without needing the guidance of others,[14] John Stuart Mill opposed paternalist interference with people for their own good, and contemporary liberals worry about welfare-dependency.[15] Sennett's view is that this liberal view is culture-specific and that dependence, in both private and public spheres, can itself be dignified.

Power as Domination

All of which leaves us with the question of how we are to understand *power as domination*. What is it that renders power over others dominating? And what is wrong with it? In what way does such power work against their interests? What would be a convincing way of showing that examples such as those in the previous paragraph are *not* instances of domination? Perhaps some of them are, or sometimes are. Perhaps we should see paternalism, where it is justified, as justified domination rather than as beneficent power: perhaps non-seat-belt-wearers just need to be dominated. Perhaps we should grant that some mothers dominate, that some therapists are manipulative and that some military officers are bullies. But what characterizes cases where subjection to power and dependency can be accepted as non-dominating is that the restrictions of choice involved are not really, or merely, invasions of freedom: they do not, in Spinoza's words, impede those subject to them from living as their 'own nature and judgment dictate'. To the contrary, in such cases, in a variety of ways, power facilitates or promotes freedom so understood. So we may conclude that power as domination is the ability to constrain the choices of others, coercing them or securing their compliance, by impeding them from living as their own nature and judgment dictate.

We have now arrived at the question addressed in *PRV*. It is an old, classical question, which we can now formulate as: how does domination work? How do the powerful secure the compliance (unwilling or willing) of those they dominate? To ask this is to ask a conceptual question and an analytical question.

The first concerns the *concept* of power itself: how are we to know when such power is at work? Here my answer is straightforward. We should search behind appearances for the hidden, least visible forms of power. To pick up the threads of the foregoing discussion, that means that the power of the powerful is to be viewed as ranging across issues and contexts, as extending to some unintended consequences and as capable of being effective even without active intervention. And, since such power consists in the ability to bring about significant outcomes, that means that power as domination will be present wherever it furthers, or does not harm, the interests of the powerful and bears negatively upon the interests of those subject to it, where 'interests' is understood across the range of the senses indicated above.

The second, analytical, question concerns the *mechanisms* by means of which such power is able to secure compliance.[16] Here it will be helpful to return to Spinoza who, having defined *potestas*, goes on to distinguish four different ways in which it manifests itself:

> One man has another in his power when he holds him in bonds; when he has disarmed him and deprived him of the means of self-defence or escape; when he has inspired him with fear; or when he has bound him so closely by a service that he would rather please his benefactor than himself, and rather be guided by his benefactor's judgment than by his own. The man who has another in his power in the first or second way holds his body only, not his mind; whereas he who controls another in the third or fourth way has made the mind as well as the body of the other subject to his right; but only while the fear or hope remains. Once the one or the other has been removed, the second man is left in possession of his own right.   (Spinoza 1958[1677]: 273–5)[17]

This passage is interesting, not least for the distinction it draws between bodily and mental bonds. Spinoza's first two ways – physical control and confinement (which I shall hence-forth treat as 'force'[18]) – differ from the second two in operating independently of *the mind*. But then Spinoza goes on to add to the second two a fifth significant way, or mechanism, of power:

> One man's power of judgment can be subject to the right of a second in another way: the first man may be the dupe of the second. This means that the mind is fully possessed of its own right, or completely free, in so far as it can use reason cor-rectly. Indeed, since as human power (*potentia*) must be judged by strength of mind rather than by vigour of body, it means that those whose reason is most powerful, and who are most guided thereby, are also the most fully possessed of their own right.   (Spinoza 1958[1677]: 275)

And elsewhere, in his *Tractatus Theologico-Politicus*, Spinoza com-ments on this further way, observing that

> a man's judgment can be influenced in many ways, some of them hardly credible; so much so, in fact, that though not directly under another's command it may depend entirely on his words, and thus in that respect can properly be called sub-ject to his right. Yet, in spite of all that political skill has been able to achieve in this field, it has never been completely suc-cessful; men have always found that individuals were full of their own ideas, and that opinions varied as much as tastes. (Spinoza 1958[1677]: 227)

In these passages Spinoza began to discuss the topic before us: namely, the various mechanisms of subjection, and in particular the last, to which I will turn in Chapter 3.

Michel Foucault, whose ideas about power I will now discuss, conceived of power as both bodily and mental and was as impressed as Spinoza both by its capacity to influence judgment and by the omnipresence of resistance to its sway, but, as we will see, his account purports to be subversive of Spinoza's belief in freedom and reason. I discuss Foucault's work on power for two reasons. The first is that it has hugely influenced our thinking about power, across many fields and disciplines, notably cultural studies, comparative literature, social history, anthropology, criminology and women's studies. The second is that Foucault's approach has been said to reveal a 'fourth dimension of power' (Digesser 1992) and taken by some to undermine the kind of approach exemplified and advocated here.

Foucault on Power: an Ultra-radical View

In the first place, I observe, in a preliminary way, that far too much of the voluminous writing about his view of power is either obscurantist when friendly or dismissive when critical. An instance of the latter is Peter Morriss's comment that, since the French word '*pouvoir*' does not capture the dispositional sense of power as ability (as in '*puissance*'), 'the widespread belief that Foucault has anything to say about power (i.e. *puissance*, or something quite close to it) is simply based on a lax translation' (Morriss 2002: xvii). For such an acute writer, this comment is surprisingly obtuse. For, as we have seen, the power of domination requires, where it is not coercive, the compliance of willing subjects. Foucault's massively influential work purports to address the rich topic of the mechanisms by which that compliance is secured.

Foucault approached this topic in an original way, with a distinctive focus of interest. In the first place, he strikingly proposed that there is a deep and intimate connection between power and knowledge, viewing these mechanisms in relation to the various applied social scientific disciplines that, so he argued, render them effective: their effectiveness, in his view, largely derives from the shaping impact on people of experts' knowledge claims. Secondly, his overall aim was to produce a 'micro-physics of power'. In explaining this idea, he wrote that 'in thinking of the mechanisms of power, I am thinking rather of its capillary forms of existence, the point where power reaches into the very grain of individuals, touches their bodies, and inserts itself into their very actions and attitudes, their discourses, learning processes, and everyday lives' (Foucault 1980a: 39). I agree with David Garland's rather precise summation of what 'power' amounts to within this conception: it is 'not to be thought of as the property of particular classes or individuals who "have" it, nor as an instrument which they can somehow "use" at will.' It refers instead to

> the various forms of domination and subordination and the asymmetrical balance of forces which operate whenever and wherever social relations exist. These power relationships, like the social relations which they invest, display no simple pattern since, for Foucault, social life is to be thought of as taking place not within a single overarching 'society', but instead across a multiplicity of fields of forces which are sometimes connected and sometimes not. His special focus is always upon the way these power relations are organized, the forms they take and the techniques they depend upon, rather than upon the groups and individuals who dominate or are dominated as a consequence.

So Foucault's concern was with 'structural relationships, institutions, strategies and techniques' rather than with 'concrete policies and the actual people they involve'. In this conception,

> power is a pervasive aspect of social life and is not limited to the sphere of formal politics or of open conflict. It is also to be thought of as productive in its effect rather than repressive in so far as power shapes the actions of individuals and harnesses their bodily powers to its ends. In this sense power operates 'through' individuals rather than 'against' them and helps constitute the individual who is at the same time its vehicle.   (Garland 1990: 138)

I do not propose to provide here yet another exposition of Foucault's account of power (of which there are more than enough[19]) but rather to assess the extent to which and the ways in which that account offers clarifying and illuminating answers to the question on which we are focusing, namely: how do the powerful secure the compliance of those they dominate? How did Foucault answer the conceptual question: in what does the power of the powerful consist and how is it to be understood? and the analytical question: how do the powerful secure compliance? Plainly, he conceived power broadly, seeking to uncover its least evident and least perceptible forms. Power, he wrote, 'is tolerable only on condition that it mask a substantial part of itself. Its success is proportional to its ability to hide its own mechanisms' (Foucault 1980c[1976]: 86). Nancy Fraser writes that 'Foucault enables us to understand power very broadly, and yet very finely, as anchored in the multiplicity of what he calls "micropractices," the social practices that constitute everyday life in modern societies' (Fraser 1989: 18). So how broad is his understanding of power and how fine-grained are his analyses of its mechanisms?

He makes a number of distinctive claims about how power is to be conceived. However, there is one key idea that can be seen as central to his so-called 'genealogical' works from the mid 1970s onwards, from the study of punishment to the history of sexuality, which analyse the emergence of modern techniques of power across various domains of social life. It is adumbrated at the beginning of *Discipline and Punish* as the first general rule guiding that work:

Do not concentrate the study of the punitive mechanisms on their 'repressive' effects alone, on their 'punishment' aspects alone, but situate them in a whole series of their possible positive effects, even if these seem marginal at first sight. As a consequence, regard punishment as a complex social function.   (Foucault 1978[1975]: 23)[20]

The idea – that power both represses and produces – is then repeatedly restated and developed, and also wildly overstated and exaggerated, in the course of the next decade in numerous studies, essays, lectures and interviews.

The idea, in its non-overstated and non-exaggerated form, is simply this: that if power is to be effective, those subject to it must be rendered susceptible to its effects.[21] Repression is 'negative', presumably, in saying 'no': it prohibits and constrains, setting limits to what agents do and might desire. 'Production' is 'positive': power in this sense 'traverses and produces things, it induces pleasure, forms knowledge, produces discourse' (Foucault 1980a: 119). More specifically, it produces 'subjects', forging their character and 'normalizing them,' rendering them capable of and willing to adhere to norms of sanity, health, sexuality and other forms of propriety. Foucault claims that these norms mould the 'soul' and are 'inscribed' upon the body; and they are maintained by policing the boundary between the normal and the abnormal and by continuous and systematic surveillance that is both inter- and intra-subjective. Ian Hacking's felicitous phrase 'making up people' captures the bare bones of this idea, together with its Foucauldian connotations (Hacking 1986). Foucault's development of this idea falls into two phases: the work on discipline and volume 1 of the *History of Sexuality,* and the subsequent writings, from 1978 to his death in 1984, on what he called 'governmentality' – a neologism referring to the ways in which in modern societies various authorities administer populations, to the ways in which individuals shape their own selves, and to the ways in which these processes get aligned.

The trouble is that, for most of his life, Foucault never ceased to clothe this idea in Nietzschean rhetoric, within which power excluded both freedom and truth. Power, he wrote, 'is coextensive with the social body; there are no spaces of primal liberty between the meshes of its network' (Foucault 1980a: 142). According to this rhetoric, there can be no liberation from power, either within a given context or across contexts; and there is no way of judging between ways of life, since each imposes its own

regime of truth, its 'general politics' of truth; that is, the types of discourse which it accepts and makes function as true, the mechanisms and instances which enable one to distinguish true and false statements, the means by which each is sanctioned; the techniques and procedures accorded value in the acquisition of truth; the status of those who are charged with saying what counts as true.   (Foucault 1980a: 38)

And so, not surprisingly, it has been claimed – and is widely supposed – that Foucault's achievement is to have undermined 'the model of the rational, autonomous moral agent'. That ideal, it would appear, 'should be seen, not as evidencing the absence of domination, but rather as one of domination's most fundamental effects', for 'power is ubiquitous and there can be no personalities that are formed independently of its effects'. If Foucault is right, then we must abandon 'the emancipatory ideal of a society in which individuals are free from the negative effects of power' and the conventional view that power can be based on the rational consent of its subjects (Hindess 1996: 149–58). If all this is so, then Foucault's view of power is indeed a *very* radical view. But is it so?

In the first phase, Foucault sees power, the power of some over others, as domination, exploring the ways in which those others, its subjects, are 'produced'. In *Discipline and Punish* they are constrained and confined and moulded into conformity – into 'docile bodies' – in ways that recall Spinoza's first two, purely physical ways of exerting *potestas*. As Garland writes,

What is meant by 'power' here is the idea of controlling – or rather 'producing' – behaviour, whether directly through the disciplinary training of offenders or, more indirectly, by way of deterrent threat and example to the general population. Punishment is thus thought of as a means of control which administers the bodies of individuals and, through them, the body politic.   (Garland 1990: 162)

Moreover, such power is, at least ideally, inactive, employing Panoptical surveillance to 'induce in the inmates a state of permanent and conscious visibility that assures the automatic functioning of power', for the perfection of power should tend to render its actual exercise unnecessary; this architectural apparatus should be a machine for creating and sustaining a power relation independent of the person who exercises it.   (Foucault 1978[1975]: 201)

The picture is one of a 'calculated manipulation' of the body's 'elements, its gestures, its behaviour'. Discipline produces

subjected and practised bodies, 'docile' bodies. Discipline increases the forces of the body (in economic terms of utility) and diminishes these same forces (in political terms of obedience) ... it turns [the body] into an 'aptitude', a 'capacity', which it seeks to increase; on the other hand, it reverses the course of the energy, the power that might result from it, and turns it into a relation of strict subjection.   (Foucault 1978[1975]: 138)

And Foucault generalizes this into an image of the 'carceral' or 'disciplinary society': is it, he asks, 'surprising that prisons resemble factories, schools, barracks, hospitals, which all resemble prisons?' (Foucault 1978[1975]: 228). All this conveys a one-sided, monolithic image of unidirectional control.[22] On this account, humanitarianism itself, as Taylor notes, 'seems to be understood as a kind of stratagem of the new growing mode of control' (Taylor 1984: 157). One reason for this one-sidedness is doubtless that Foucault was, characteristically, not investigating actual disciplinary practices but their *design*. His purpose was to portray their idealized form – describing not how they work, or ever worked, but an ideal type of how they are meant to work.[23] As he himself wrote, the Panopticon was the

diagram of a mechanism of power reduced to its ideal form; its functioning, abstracted from any obstacle, resistance or friction, must be represented as a pure architectural and optical system: it is in fact a figure of political technology that may or must be detached from any specific use.   (Foucault 1978 [1975]: 205)

With the *History of Sexuality* this portrayal of domination gives way to a less reductive and 'physicalist', but no less ideal-typical and unidirectional, account of the rise of 'bio-power' in which the deployment of sexuality became part of the 'great technology of power in the nineteenth century' – a 'life-administering power' concerned with using social science and statistics to 'normalize', control and regulate the life and health of populations. Here, as with discipline, the 'productive' role of power in 'making up people' is simply the obverse of its repressive role, but we are given a phenomenologically richer account of what is involved. Thus we may think we gain more freedom by casting off sexual inhibitions, but we are in fact dominated by images of what constitutes a healthy, fulfilled human being. Sexual permissiveness is an illusory freedom because we are controlled by an

> economic (and also perhaps ideological) exploitation of eroticization, from sun-tan products to pornographic films. Responding precisely to the revolt of the body, we find a new mode of investment which presents itself no longer in the form of control by repression but that of control by stimulation. 'Get undressed – but be slim, be good-looking, tanned!'
>
> (Foucault 1980a: 57)

And consider the ritual of the confession, in which, according to Foucault, from 'the Christian penance to the present day, sex was a privileged theme' (Foucault 1980c[1976]: 61). As Amy Allen observes,

> Power operates in and through the practice of confession both to subject individuals to the injunction to tell the truth about their sexuality and to enable them to take up the position of sexual subject. (Allen 1999: 36)

The confession, according to Foucault, is 'a ritual that unfolds within a power relationship', for

> one does not confess without the presence (or virtual presence) of a partner who is not simply the interlocutor but the

authority who requires the confession, prescribes and appreci-
ates it, and intervenes in order to judge, punish, forgive, con-
sole, and reconcile; a ritual in which the truth is corroborated
by the obstacles and resistances it has had to surmount in
order to be formulated; and finally, a ritual in which the
expression alone, independently of its external consequences,
produces intrinsic modifications in the person who articulates it: it exonerates, redeems and purifies him; it unburdens
him of his wrongs, liberates him, and promises him salvation.
(Foucault 1980c[1976]: 61–2)

And Foucault writes of the 'immense labour to which the
West has submitted generations in order to produce ... men's
subjection: their constitution as subjects in both senses of the
word' (Foucault 1980c[1976]: 60).

This last point, and the pun which expresses it, perfectly captures his central idea in this, the first phase of his explicit writings
about power: the subject is 'constituted' through subjection
(*assujetissement*) to power.[24] Unsurprisingly, this claim has been
the target of widespread critical discussion and accusations of a
structuralist commitment to determinism. What scope, critics
have asked, does this picture leave for the agency of the subject?
Do not human agents, in Kenny's phrase, have two-way powers?
At this stage, Foucault gave a very abstract answer:

Where there is power, there is resistance, and yet, or rather
consequently, this resistance is never in a position of exterior-
ity in relation to power.   (Foucault 1980c[1976]: 95)

Yet, as Allen rightly observes, this is merely to posit the conceptual necessity of resistance, as itself 'internal' to, and so generated by, power:

He never offers a detailed account of resistance as an empirical phenomenon in any of his genealogical analyses. The
only social actors in these works are the dominating agents;
there is no discussion of the strategies employed by madmen,

delinquents, schoolchildren, perverts, or 'hysterical' women to modify or contest the disciplinary or bio-power exercised over them.   (Allen 1999: 54)[25]

As if to answer such criticisms, Foucault's subsequent writings on the theme of 'governmentality' strike a more voluntaristic note. In 'The Subject and Power', power is said to be 'exercised only over free subjects, and only insofar as they are free. By this we mean individual or collective subjects who are faced with a field of possibilities in which several ways of behaving, several reactions and diverse comportments may be realized' (Foucault 1982: 221). 'Governmentality' is an influential Foucauldian idea with a multiple reference. First, to 'rationalities of rule' – styles of reasoning embodied in governing practices. Second, to conceptions of the person that they seek to inculate – such as the active citizen, the consumer, the enterprising subject, the psychiatric outpatient, and so on. Third, to 'technologies of the self' – that individuals deploy as they pursue their respective interests, acting upon themselves to induce virtuous habits and fashion their characters. And fourth, to the ways in which these elements are aligned with one another. So this version of 'making up people' is supposed to preserve their freedom, indeed to exhibit governing through freedom. By 'governmentality', Foucault stated,

I am aiming at the totality of practices, by which one can constitute, define, organize, instrumentalize the strategies which individuals in their liberty can have in regard to each other.   (Foucault 1987: 19)

So how are we now to understand the Foucauldian idea of power 'constituting' the subject? The 'Final Foucault's' answer to this question is instructive: 'the subject constitutes himself in an active fashion, by the practices of self'. These practices are 'not something the individual invents by himself' but 'patterns that he finds in the culture and which are proposed, suggested and imposed on him by his culture, his society and his social group' (Foucault 1987: 11).

But with this answer the ultra-radicalism of Foucault's view of power dissolves. For it amounts to restating some elementary sociological commonplaces. Individuals are socialized: they are oriented to roles and practices that are culturally and socially given; they internalize these and may experience them as freely chosen; indeed, their freedom may, as Durkheim liked to say, be the fruit of regulation – the outcome of disciplines and controls. Of course, it restates these truths in a distinctively Foucauldian way, by suggesting that these socialization practices could be otherwise, that they link up with wider forms of rule, that they should be seen as forms of 'government' outside the state and that such 'governing' is done by employers, administrative authorities, social workers, parents, schoolteachers, medical personnel and experts of all kinds. These non-state authorities propose, suggest and impose these roles and practices upon individuals – that is, agents with two-way powers – who, in turn, must interpret their requirements and will sometimes resist and sometimes reject them. But all of this means that criteria will be needed to decide where their power amounts to domination and, in general, to distinguish between dominating and non-dominating power and dependency. And, not surprisingly, the 'Final Foucault' reaches for just such a distinction and so ends up travelling down the path sketched in the conceptual map above. Thus he asserts that

we must distinguish the relationships of power as strategic games between liberties – strategic games that result in the fact that some people try to determine the conduct of others – and the states of domination, which are what we ordinarily call power. And between the two, between the games of power and the states of domination, you have governmental technologies – giving the term a very wide meaning for it is also the way in which you govern your wife, your children, as well as the way you govern an institution. (Foucault 1987: 19)[26]

And for Foucault domination now exists where 'the relations of power are fixed in such a way that they are perpetually asymmetrical and the margin of liberty is extremely limited'. The problem, he now says, is to allow the games of power 'to be played with a minimum of domination' (Foucault 1987: 12, 18).

In sum, Foucault's first way of interpreting the key idea central to his view of power – that power is 'productive' through the social construction of subjects, rendering the governed governable – made no sense.[27] Taking this to mean that those subject to power are 'constituted' by it is best read as a striking overstatement deployed in his purely ideal-typical depictions of disciplinary and bio-power, not as an analysis of the extent to which the various modern forms of power he identified actually succeed, or fail, in securing the compliance of those subject to it. Indeed, for all his talk of 'micro-physics', 'analytics' and 'mechanisms', Foucault was a genealogist, concerned with the historical recovery of the formation of norms (such as define the mad, the sick, the criminal and the abnormal) and as such he had no interest in analysing such mechanisms by examining variation, outcomes and effects: he just asserted that there were such effects. And yet Foucault's writings have had an extraordinarily wide impact, encouraging scholars in many fields and disciplines to engage in just such an analysis – analysing fields of practices that he identified, by putting, so to speak, his dramatically exaggerated ideal types to empirical work, by asking, precisely, just *how* and *to what extent* the governed are rendered governable. I do not think it altogether fanciful to suggest that Foucault's writings thereby themselves exhibit an interesting kind of power: the power of seduction. In Foucault's case – and there are others in the history of the human sciences[28] – this has been a singularly productive power, generating a remarkable quantity of important and interesting empirical work that, arguably, constitutes what Imre Lakatos might have called a successful and progressive research programme. In the light of this last suggestion, I conclude this discussion by addressing the question of the fine-grainedness of the Foucauldian contribution to analysing power's mechanisms by citing some examples, not from him but from work inspired by his ideas.

Foucault Applied:
The Securing of Voluntary Compliance

Consider, first, Foucault's idea of disciplinary power. Whereas Foucault vividly portrays the *design* of Bentham's Panopticon, others have investigated the impact of prisons on inmates, and their varied reactions and, more widely, of Panoptical principles on people. So Foucault wrote:

> He who is subjected to a field of visibility, and who knows it, assumes responsibility for the constraints of power; he inscribes in himself the power relations in which he simultaneously plays both roles; he becomes the principle of his own subjection. (Foucault 1978[1975]: 202–3)

Sandra Bartky puts this idea to work in analysing one aspect of the contemporary subjection of women. It is, she writes,

> women who practice this discipline on and against their own bodies. ... The woman who checks her make-up half a dozen times a day to see if her foundation has caked or her mascara has run, who worries that the wind or rain may spoil her hairdo, who looks frequently to see if her stockings have bagged at the ankle, or who, feeling fat, monitors everything she eats, has become, just as surely as the inmate of the Panopticon, a self-policing subject, a self committed to a relentless self-surveillance. This self-surveillance is a form of obedience to patriarchy. (Bartky 1990: 80)

In her remarkable book *Unbearable Weight* Susan Bordo quotes Foucault's claim that in self-surveillance

there is no need for arms, physical violence, material constraints. Just a gaze. An inspecting gaze, a gaze which each
individual under its weight will end by interiorising to the
point that he is his own overseer, each individual thus exercising this surveillance over, and against himself.   (Foucault
1980a: 155).

Although female submission often involves coercion, Bordo
finds that these ideas illuminate the politics of appearance. She
writes that

they have been extremely helpful both to my analysis of the
contemporary disciplines of diet and exercise and to my
understanding of eating disorders as arising out of and reproducing normative feminine practices of our culture, practices
which train the female body in docility and obedience to cultural demands while at the same time being *experienced* in
terms of power and control. Within a Foucauldian framework, power and pleasure do not cancel each other. Thus,
the heady experience of feeling powerful or 'in control', far
from being a necessarily accurate reflection of one's social
position, is always suspect as itself the product of power relations whose shape may be very different.   (Bordo 2003: 27)

Bordo notes that in his later writings Foucault emphasized
that 'power relations are never seamless but are always spawn-
ing new forms of culture and subjectivity, new opportunities for
transformation', and that he came to see that where there is
power there is also resistance. But transformations of dominant
forms and institutions can also occur through conformity to prevailing norms: so, for example,

the woman who goes into a rigorous weight-training program
in order to achieve the currently stylish look may discover
that her new muscles give her the self-confidence that enables
her to assert herself more forcefully at work. Modern power-
relations are thus unstable; resistance is perpetual and hegemony precarious.   (Bordo 2003: 28)

Or consider Jacques Donzelot's study of 'the policing of families' which he describes as analysing what the 'work of Michel Foucault has succeeded in identifying', namely,

> the biopolitical dimension: the proliferation of political technologies that invested the body, health, modes of subsistence and lodging – the entire space of existence in European countries from the eighteenth century onwards. (Donzelot 1979: 6)

Donzelot's analysis combines the various Foucauldian elements: expert knowledge, drawn on by a 'tutelary complex' of social workers, doctors, philanthropists, psychiatrists, feminists, birth-control campaigners and so on, applied in capillary fashion across society in schools, hospitals, social work offices, clinics, juvenile courts, and engaged in 'normalizing' both bourgeois and working-class families, albeit in different ways, through monitoring and exhortation. Thus,

> [t]he family climate, the social context that causes a particular child to become a 'risk,' will be thoroughly studied. The catalogue of these indications makes it possible to encompass all forms of maladjustment, so as to construct a second circle of prevention. Starting from a desire to reduce appeals to the judiciary and reliance on the penal system, social work would depend on a psychiatric, sociological and psychoanalytic knowledge for support, hoping to forestall the drama of police action by replacing the secular arm of the law with the extended hand of the educator.

Donzelot treats the family as both 'governed' and 'governing', in ways that vary across historical time periods. From outside, it is shaped by the economy, the law, the franchise and so on, whereas within, parents socialize children, mothers civilize fathers, and so on. These changing internal relations are affected by external interventions. In the late nineteenth century, medical and educational reformers, charity workers and philanthropists, seeking to improve the welfare of the family's children, would enlist and empower the mother/wife *vis-à-vis* the father/husband; and she, seeking the best for her children and to advance the family status, would be a willing ally, taking her cues from the experts. In this way Donzelot pursues the Foucauldian theme of the linkage between the normalizaton of individuals, who conform to socially structured norms as they pursue their several interests, and the bio-political control of populations, promoting national efficiency, the health of the population, the control of the birth rate and the control of crime. The modern 'tutelary complex' involves a new form of power with greater range and penetration, in which the old criminal law, invoking prohibition and punishment, is combined with new expert norms concerning health, psychology, hygiene and so on: 'the substitution of the educative for the judicial can also be interpreted as an extension of the judicial, a refinement of its methods, an endless ramification of its powers' (Donzelot 1979: 97, 98). The whole network of family, school, health visitor, philanthropist and juvenile court functions largely by co-operation rather than coercion, exercising more control with more legitimacy but in the absence of any single overall strategy or set of coherent aims. The policing of families differs, however, according to social class. Working-class families are more liable to be delinquent, to be claimants and to constitute problems and thus require external attention and compulsory intervention; bourgeois families are, Donzelot suggests (with Foucauldian irony), 'freer' in being more conformist, self-disciplined and self-policing.

I conclude with two further Foucault-inspired analyses of the securing of voluntary compliance through non-obvious mechanisms. One is an extremely fine-grained case study of politics, administration and planning in the Danish town of Aalborg in Northern Jutland by Bent Flyvbjerg (Flyvbjerg 1998). Assuming that concentrating 'on the most visible aspects of power . . . results in an incomplete and biased picture of power relations', this study recounts how the award-winning 'Aalborg Project', designed to 'substantially restructure and democratically improve the down-town environment, was transformed . . . into environmental degradation and social distortion'. Flyvbjerg shows how institutions that were 'supposed to represent what they themselves called "the public interest"' were 'deeply embedded in the hidden exercise of power and the protection of special interests' (Flyvbjerg 1998: 231, 225). His close examination of how the location of Aalborg's bus terminal gets decided focuses on 'the strategy and tactics of power in relation to rationality', taking power to be 'the ability to facilitate or suppress knowledge' (Flyvbjerg 1998: 36). By providing 'thick description', from the various actors' perspectives, of the project's journey from genesis to design to political ratification, implementation and operation, finally dissolving into an 'impasse', Flyvbjerg succeeds in revealing how powerfully placed actors[29] frame issues, present information and structure arguments and how the less powerful and the powerless either acquiesce in or feebly resist a process which culminates in most people ending up worse off.[30] The story involves the occasional exercise of 'raw power', where 'actions are dictated by whatever works best to defeat an opponent', but mostly describes the ways in which 'surveys, analysis, documentation, and technical argumentation are ... used to try and create consensus' but are also 'attempts to avoid confrontation, such avoidance ... being a characteristic of stable relations' (Flyvbjerg 1998: 141). The detailed analysis is fascinating, but its author spices it with dramatic Foucault-esque pronouncements. 'Rationality,' he asserts, 'is context-dependent; the context of rationality is power; and power blurs the dividing line between rationality and rationalization.' Rationality is 'penetrated by power, and it becomes meaningless, or misleading – for politicians, administrators, and researchers alike – to operate with a concept of rationality in which power is absent.' (Here, following Foucault himself, Flyvbjerg is criticizing Jürgen Habermas.[31]) Indeed, and most succinctly, power 'determines what counts as knowledge, what kind of interpretation attains authority as the dominant interpretation' (Flyvbjerg 1998: 97, 227, 226).

And consider, finally, Clarissa Hayward's case for 'de-facing power',[32] which argues against thinking of power as implying an account of freedom in which 'action is independently chosen and/or authentic' and in favour of defining it as 'a network of boundaries that delimit, for all, the field of what is socially possible' (Hayward 2000: 3–4). She thus advances a direct challenge to the kind of view espoused in the present volume, and to the so-called 'power debate' generally, and she does so, in part, through a detailed and subtle ethnographic study of two schools in Connecticut. Her book is largely Foucault-inspired[33] and it simultaneously exhibits, in my view, both the analytical virtues such inspiration can impart to empirical work and the seductive power it can exercise over those inclined to theorize about power (see Lukes 2002). Her study of the two schools centres on 'patterned asymmetries in the way institutions and practices shape pedagogic possibility' (Hayward 2000: 56). One school, North End Community School, serves a relatively poor, largely black urban neighbourhood. There is an 'emphasis on discipline, and specifically on obedience to authority', pupils are 'monitored and barraged with a series of reprimands and punishments for rule violations that range from the routine and trivial to the potentially serious', and the teachers focus on inculcating 'survival skills' and avoiding the dangers and lures of 'the street'. The other school, Fair View, serves a white, upper-middle-class suburban community of upper-level managers and professionals. Here, in a socially exclusive environment, the teachers engage in what might appear to be 'empowering the children of those who, by virtue of their social position have power in contemporary American society'. The pupils have 'an active, at times almost confrontational engagement' with authority, they are enabled to 'participate in rule-making', they 'direct their own conduct and, with insistent care . . . mould their own characters' (Hayward 2000: 67, 98, 117, 116, 134). She shows how at North End the external constraints lead the teachers to favour tough, authoritarian practices that are, however, locally enabling, since trust and obedience to authority and rule following provide short-term protection against harm from 'the street', while at Fair View the effect is to reproduce exclusionary social and racial stereotypes and an unquestioning view of a 'sanctified' and de-politicized learning process. She is concerned to deny that Fair View's teachers are powerful and that their pedagogy is 'empowering'. Her point is to deny that power is distributed among agents and to argue, instead, that it operates impersonally by shaping 'the field of the possible' (ibid., p. 118) So she asserts that *both* sets of teachers and pupils are equally constrained by such (de-faced) power, with circumscribed possibilities and pedagogic options. Thus she claims that

> First, depoliticized standards of conduct and character, ends of learning, and social identities, which help define power relations at Fair View, are as firm limits to action as are the hierarchically imposed and enforced rules at North End. Second, transgressions of these limits are punished at least as severely, if not more so, at Fair View. And third, the depoliticization of key norms, identities and other boundaries defining pedagogic practices at Fair View reproduces and reinforces inequalities, both within and beyond the bounds of community. (Hayward 2000: 67, 98, 117, 116, 134, 9)

But norms can be both constraining and liberating. Of course, on Hayward's account, there are powerful constraining norms at work at Fair View but they are norms that encourage pupils to criticize rules and confront authority. Focusing only on the impersonal constraints on teachers and pupils alike renders her blind to or, better, silent about, the multiple freedoms their powerful social positions afford them.

The trouble is that Hayward links this careful ethnography to her version of the ultra-radical Foucauldian view of power as denying the very possibility of distinguishing 'between free action and action shaped by the action of others' (Hayward 2000: 15). Her claim is that

> any definition of the line dividing free action from action that is, in part [sic.], the product of power's exercise itself serves the political function of privileging as natural, chosen or true some realm of social action. (Hayward 2000: 29)

For, once one acknowledges

> that identity itself is a product of power relations, that fields
> of action are necessarily bound, for example, through pro-
> cesses of acculturation and identity formation, it becomes
> necessary to reject a view of power that presupposes the possi-
> bility of distinguishing free action from action shaped by the
> action of others. The ways people act – how they conduct
> themselves, think, feel, perceive, reason, what people value,
> how they define themselves in relation to communities to
> which they experience themselves as belonging – are in signif-
> icant part [sic.] the effect of social action. To define as 'free' a
> given set of wants, social needs, capacities, beliefs, disposi-
> tions, or behaviors is to exclude from analysis a priori a host
> of ways in which human freedom is shaped. (Hayward
> 2000: 30)

As the reader can see, these quotations themselves express
hesitation ('in part', 'in significant part') in enunciating the
ultra-radical view: that power 'constitutes' the 'free' subject.
None of the accompanying ethnography requires or justifies it
and indeed, as we have seen, Foucault himself in the end wisely
retreated from it.

I have cited these various examples (from among countless
others) of Foucault-inspired work with two purposes. The first
is to show that they begin to explore subtle forms of the securing
of willing compliance, in which people are enlisted into wider
patterns of normative control, often acting as their own 'over-
seers', while believing themselves, sometimes falsely, to be free
of power, making their own choices, pursuing their own interests, assessing arguments rationally and coming to their own
conclusions. The second purpose is to suggest that none of these
works supports the extravagant claims made by Foucault and
too many others that his thought offers an ultra-radical view of
power that has profoundly subversive implications for how we

are to think about freedom and rationality.[34] Should they lead us to conclude that we are all subjected subjects, 'constituted' by power, that the modern individual is the 'effect' of power, that power needs to be 'de-faced', that rationality is 'context-dependent' and 'penetrated' by power, that power cannot be based on rational consent – in short, that after Foucault it no longer makes sense to speak, with Spinoza, of the very possibility of people being more or less free from others' power to live as their own nature and judgment dictate? In the next chapter, I assume that it does make sense and offer some suggestions as to what sense it makes.

3

THREE-DIMENSIONAL POWER

PRV, first published as a short book some thirty years ago in the context of an ongoing debate, makes several contentious claims in an extremely brief compass. It offers a definition of the concept of power, claiming both that the concept is 'essentially contested' and that the conceptual analysis proposed is superior to those criticized; and it claims to provide a way of analysing power that goes deeper and is at once value-laden, theoretical and empirical. As indicated, these claims face a series of difficulties and objections (not least that they are mutually incompatible) that many critics have pressed and pursued. In considering these claims, difficulties and objections, the question before us is: what in the foregoing presentation, reproduced as Chapter 1 of this volume, is to be abandoned, what qualified, what defended and what developed further?

In this chapter I shall, first, resume what has already been suggested concerning the specificity of power as domination within the wider conceptual field of power in general and defend focusing on power in this sense. Second, I will ask whether it is plausible to think that we can arrive at an uncontested way of understanding it and argue that, because of its links with no less contested notions of freedom, authenticity, autonomy and real interests, it is not. Third, I will defend the claim that power has a third dimension — securing the consent to domination of willing subjects — against two kinds of objection: that such consent is non-existent or very rare, and that it cannot be secured. Finally, I will argue that conceiving of power in this way cannot dispense with a defensible understanding of the notions of 'real interests' and 'false consciousness'.

The Definition of Power

In the first place, as already adumbrated in Chapter 2, the definition of 'the underlying concept of power' offered in Section 5 of *PRV* is, plainly, entirely unsatisfactory in several respects. Following others in the 'power debate', it focuses on the *exercise* of power, thereby committing the 'exercise fallacy': power is a dispositional concept, identifying an ability or capacity, which may or may not be exercised. Secondly, it focuses entirely on the exercise of 'power over' — the power of some A over some B and B's condition of dependence on A. Thirdly, it equates such dependence-inducing power with *domination*, assuming that 'A affects B in a manner contrary to B's interests', thereby neglecting what we have seen to be the manifold ways in which power over others can be productive, transformative, authoritative and compatible with dignity. Fourthly, assuming that power, thus defined, affects the interests of those subject to it adversely, it offers no more than the most perfunctory and questionable account of what such interests are and, moreover, it treats an actor's interests as unitary, failing to consider differences, interactions and conflicts among one's interests. And, finally, it operates (like much of the literature on power) with a reductive and simplistic picture of binary power relations, an unending array of permutating relations between A and B, as if it were obvious that Lenin was right to say that the only important question is 'Who whom?' Perhaps it is and he was, but we need to broaden and deepen the scope of the analysis.

What is clear is that the underlying concept here defined is not 'power' but rather the securing of compliance to domination.

The text addresses the question: 'how do the powerful secure the compliance of those they dominate?' – a narrower question than that suggested by its snappy title. On the other hand, it can be argued that the question addressed is not without interest, even if it is an exaggeration to claim that this is the central meaning of power as traditionally understood, and that the concerns it expresses are those that have always centrally preoccupied students of power. Yet, it *has*, after all, preoccupied many of them, from La Boétie and Hobbes to Foucault and Bourdieu, and it is, I submit, worth trying to answer it.

Essential Contestedness

But can it be answered? More precisely, is it susceptible of an objectively determinable answer, such that all reasonable persons will converge in agreeing to its truth?

There are, as suggested in Chapter 2, disagreements over how widely to extend the concept of power. Should attributions of power range across issues and contexts (actual and potential), and if so which? Should they cover unintended consequences and inaction? Disagreements over these questions typically stem from methodological concerns. How are we to determine which counterfactuals are relevant? How do you decide which unintended consequences to consider? How do you study inaction and its consequences? Of course, such concerns can be met by making a series of definitional decisions. 'Power' can be given a specific meaning, tying it, for example, as many do, to intention and positive action, and other labels can be used for other meanings. Some, for example, think that if others can further my interests without my either intending or intervening to bring this about, we should speak not of my power but of my luck (Barry 1989: 270–302, and Dowding 1996). I maintain, in contrast, that such cases may, but also may not, be among the most effective and sometimes the most insidious forms of power. I continue to think that the components of the broader concept of power are researchable and that there are better reasons for seeing power in an all-embracing way than for not doing so.

The plot thickens, however, when we turn to the question of how to identify and compare overall power, for, as we have seen, this involves judging the significance of the outcomes that the powerful can bring about. As we saw, comparing the power of different agents across different sets of issues unavoidably involves judgments about the extent to which and ways in which their power furthers their own interests and/or affects the interests of others. This, I argued, is inherently controversial and involves taking sides in moral and political controversies. Determining who has more power, and how much more they have, is inseparable from assessing the significance of the impact of their power – that is, its impact on the interests of those affected. Here again, one could resolve the problem by just defining power narrowly and calling what is excluded something else.

So, for instance, one could just agree to call one-dimensional power 'power' (attributed to those who prevail in decision-making situations) and two-dimensional power 'agenda control'. But, here again, I continue to hold that the latter is best seen as a further and more basic form of power – the power to decide what is decided – for the reason that its impact on interests is measured not just by reference to express preferences but also to grievances that have not reached expression in the political arena, and that it is illuminating to say that power can be at work in preventing them for doing so. And by the same reasoning, I continue to think that it makes best sense to see some ways of averting both conflict and grievance through the securing of consent as a further dimension of power.

Further complexities arise when we come to study the mechanisms that secure compliance to domination. For the question now arises of how we are to recognize domination. Who is to say who is dominated and on what basis?

One classical answer to this question is Max Weber's. Weber defined domination as 'the probability that a command with a given specific content will be obeyed by a given group of persons' and added that 'the existence of domination turns only on the actual presence of one person successfully issuing orders to others' (Weber 1978[1910–14]: 53). For Weber domination was legitimate, that is, recognized as legitimate by those subject to it (he had no interest in illegitimate power). The trouble with this definition, from our point of view, is that it does not limit the idea of domination to subjection or subjugation-inducing acquiescence, where power is an imposition or constraint, working against the interests of those subject to it. Weber's concept is compatible with a wide range of positive power relations to which the dominated may willingly comply and from which they and others benefit overall. As Ian Shapiro has noted,

> Compliance is often compelled in armies, firms, sports teams, families, schools and countless other institutions. Indeed, political theorists from Plato to Foucault have often noted that the ineradicably hierarchical character of much social life makes power relations ubiquitous to human interaction. But this does not mean that domination is. ... Hierarchical relations are often legitimate, and, when they are, they do not involve domination.

Because of this, Shapiro conceives of domination as 'arising only from the illegitimate exercise of power'. But that will not suit our purpose either. For, as Shapiro admits, what he calls the 'faces-of-power debate' has led to the conclusion that 'domination can result from a person's or a group's shaping agendas, constraining options, and, in the limiting case, influencing people's preferences and desires' (Shapiro 2003: 53). But if that is so, then the 'limiting case' surely poses a problem, for it implies that domination can influence whom and what people recognize as legitimate. But Shapiro's definition, if it implies that legitimacy is relative to prevalent norms and beliefs, fails to capture such cases – cases, that is, where the dominated accord legitimacy to those who dominate them.[1]

So I return to my question: who is to say who is dominated, and on what basis? Sometimes the answer to this question is, in practice, non-contentious. Are slavery, serfdom, apartheid and

caste subordination forms of domination? No one these days ser-
iously doubts that they are, not least because they are openly
coercive. They involve compulsory appropriation of labour,
goods and services from a subordinate population, the latter's
subordination being fixed by birth and largely inescapable, and
all this is justified in terms of ideologies that proclaim their
immutable inferiority, confirmed and reaffirmed by law and in
public rituals. But is domination at issue in Foucault's confes-
sional, among Sandra Bartky's and Susan Bordo's women who
may practise 'discipline on and against their own bodies' yet
experience 'power and control', among Donzelot's self-policing
bourgeois mothers, in Flyvbjerg's ever more traffic-ridden Aalborg, and in Crenson's polluted Gary, Indiana, and in Hayward's contrasting schools whose teachers cannot escape
socializing their pupils into their respective prevailing norms?

One thing is clear: this is not a straightforwardly factual
question. Answering it requires taking a view about how to
interpret the meaning of acquiescence: how to determine when
it signifies compliance to power as domination. I am not just
referring to the classic hermeneutic or interpretive problem
that, as James Scott puts it, 'there is no satisfactory way to establish definitively some bedrock reality or truth behind any set of
social acts' (Scott 1990: 4). Here the question is how to know
whether the language of domination is or is not appropriate.
To speak of power as domination is to suggest the imposition of
some significant constraint upon an agent or agents' desires,
purposes or interests, which it frustrates, prevents from fulfil-
ment or even from being formulated. Power, in this sense, thus
marks a distinction between an imposition, thus understood,
and other influences. (It is just this distinction that Foucault's
Nietzschean rhetoric obscures). Charles Taylor has helped to
clarify this essential point:

If some external agency or situation wreaks some change in
me that in no way lies athwart some such desire/purpose/
aspiration/interest, then there is no call to speak of an exercise
of power/domination. Take the phenomenon of imprinting.

In human life, it also exists after a fashion. We generally come to like the foods that have assuaged our hunger, those we are fed as children in our culture. Is this an index of the domination of our culture over us? The word would lose all useful profile, would have no more distinctiveness, if we let it roam this wide. (Taylor 1984: 173)

I suggest that one way to capture this is to see the concept of domination as adding to the notion of power over others the further claim that those subject to it are rendered *less free*, in Spinoza's phrase, *to live as their nature and judgment dictate.*

Let us begin with the idea of being 'less free'. Identifying degrees of freedom cannot escape deciding among rival views of what constitute invasions or infringements of freedom, which in turn derive from rival views of what freedom is. Among such views, for example, is the idea that freedom is non-interference with the realization of people's preferences, whatever they happen to be. On this view, I am free to the extent that nobody prevents me, or (on a wider interpretation) can prevent me, from doing whatever I may prefer to do. If you think this way about freedom, then how my preferences are formed, how my judgments are made and what influences them – none of this has any bearing on the extent of my freedom. My 'nature' is simply an array of given preferences as revealed by my choices, and my 'judgment' is whatever I choose: judgments are revealed by preferences and preferences by behaviour in situations of choice. There are various ways of criticizing this picture,[2] of which the most relevant to the present discussion is this. On the suggested view of freedom, how my preferences are formed is irrelevant: all that counts is that no one hampers their realization. Such a view excludes 'a critical scrutiny of preference and desire that would reveal the many ways in which habit, fear, low expectations, and unjust background conditions deform people's choices and even their wishes for their own lives' (Nussbaum 2000: 114). But is it plausible to deny that it also matters that the preferences are *mine*, that one measure of my freedom is the extent to which I am in control of my choices and am the author of the way my life goes – which can, of course, mean conforming willingly to prevailing norms and tradition? Nevertheless, one widely accepted view of freedom is this straightforward and simple view: that people are free to the extent that nobody interferes with their doing whatever they prefer at any given moment. Call this the *minimal* view of freedom.[3]

Spinoza's formula enables us to see what is at issue here, for it can be given various interpretations that go beyond the minimal view, not all of which are mutually compatible. Here I can only sketch what is involved in the different ways there are of answering the question: 'What do my nature and my judgment dictate?', among which Spinoza's own way is only one. The formula plausibly suggests that we think of freedom as autonomy (broadly understood), that is as invoking the ideas of *authenticity* (being true to one's nature or 'self') and *autonomy* (more narrowly understood – thinking for oneself). On Spinoza's own account, living (authentically) according to the dictates of one's nature and (autonomously) according to the dictates of one's judgment is to be *rational*. Subjection to domination impedes the subject's ability 'to use reason correctly': 'those whose reason is most powerful, and who are most guided thereby, are also the most possessed of their own right' (Spinoza 1958[1677]: 275) (for 'right' read 'freedom'). This certainly captures some intuitively recognizable mechanisms of power, as well as others less obvious. Power can be deployed to block or impair its subjects' capacity to reason well, not least by instilling and sustaining misleading or illusory ideas of what is 'natural' and what sort of life their distinctive 'nature' dictates,[4] and, in general, by stunting or blunting their capacity for rational judgment. Power can induce or encourage failures of rationality. Or, to speak the robust (and sexist) seventeenth-century language of Spinoza, where one man's power of judgment is subject to another, 'the first man may be the dupe of the second'.

But to admit this is only to raise a host of further questions. For what *is* a failure of rationality? Are there alternative rationalities, internal to different historical periods or cultures, or even sub-cultures, alternative criteria for what counts as a reason, or a good reason for believing or doing something, or alternative logics or alternative 'styles of reasoning'? Or is there, as Vico thought,

> a mental language, common to all the nations, which uniformly grasps the substance of things feasible in human social life and expresses it with as many diverse modifications as these same things have diverse aspects?   (Vico 1963[1744]: 115)

Or is there, rather, given cultural diversity, nevertheless a shared basis, or inter-cultural bridgehead, 'a massive central core' (in Strawson's phrase) 'of human thinking which has no history' (Strawson 1959: 10)? And, assuming that we can give some objective, non-relative meaning to 'failures of rationality'(such as, for instance, self-deception and wishful thinking, succumbing to cognitive biases, fallacies and illusions, and to errors that depend on how issues and questions are framed; ignorance of the principles of statistical inference, and so on), to what are they attributable? How are they to be understood: as internally generated or as externally activated and sustained? The most plausible view is, of course, that they are both: that everyone is susceptible to such failures, that one can be schooled, and school oneself, to avoid them but that others are able, indeed these days employ entire phalanxes of skilled professionals, experts in communication and public relations, to benefit from their continuance. From the ancient arts of rhetoric to the contemporary skills of publicists and propagandists, it is undeniable that, as Spinoza remarked, a 'man's judgment can be influenced in many ways, some of them hardly credible'.

But the 'dictates of one's judgment' need not just involve rationality. For 'judgment' can also be taken in an Aristotelian way to mean *phronesis*, or practical wisdom involving the application of principles to particular circumstances. It is a virtue whose presence gives evidence of maturity. Here, too, we can raise the question of cultural relativity (to what extent is what counts as such wisdom and maturity culturally variable? Is there a trans-cultural way of assessing good judgment?), but, supposing that we can agree about when it is present and when it is lacking, it is clear that it is a virtue that can be cultivated or discouraged. Domination can consist in its being suppressed and stifled within relations between groups, as in colonial settings (as explored by Fanon), in authoritarian families and tyrannical educational institutions, and between individuals in asymmetrical relationships (such as that between Torvald and Nora in Ibsen's *A Doll's House*) – power relations which disempower by infantilizing.

What about the 'dictates of one's nature'? It is no longer fashionable to speak of individuals or of groups of individuals as having 'natures': to do so is to commit the unforgivable sin of essentialism. What is at issue here is, obviously, not pre-socialized or biologically given natures in the case of individuals, or the primordial natures of ethnic or racial or national groups. One way to understand domination as an imposition or constraint upon the dictates of one's nature is to interpret the latter from the standpoint of a theory of *human nature*. Here the central question is: what are the necessary conditions for human beings to flourish? What, as Marx might have put the question, are the preconditions for human beings to live in a truly human way (see Geras 1983, Lukes 1985)? What this question asks for is an account of the material and social circumstances that must obtain to enable people to live lives that meet certain normative standards: lives fit for human beings, who are treated and treat one another as ends, have equal dignity and an equal entitlement to shape their own lives, making their own choices and developing their gifts in reciprocal relations with others. The most promising contemporary attempt to work out such an account is the so-called 'capabilities approach', developed, in slightly different versions, by Amartya Sen and Martha Nussbaum (Sen 1984, 1985, 1992, 2002, Nussbaum 2000, and Nussbaum and Sen 1993). The 'intuitive idea' behind this approach is that 'certain functions are particularly central to human life, in the sense that their presence or absence is typically understood to be a mark of the presence or absence of human life', and that, as both Marx and Aristotle held, human beings are distinguished from animals in being self-directed: in being able to shape their lives 'in cooperation and reciprocity with others, rather than being passively shaped or pushed around by the world in the manner of a "flock" or "herd" animals'. A human life is distinctively human by virtue of being 'shaped throughout by these human powers of practical reason and sociability'. The claim is that 'we can arrive at an enumeration of central elements of truly human functioning that can command a broad cross-cultural consensus'[5] and, furthermore, that

> these capabilities can be convincingly argued to be of central importance in any human life, whatever else the person pursues or chooses. The central capabilities are not just instrumental to further pursuits: they are held to have value in themselves, in making the life that includes them fully human. (Nussbaum 2000: 72, 74)

If this can be convincingly argued, it gives an objective sense to the 'dictates of nature' and thereby to what counts as domination. Domination occurs where the power of some affects the interests of others by restricting their capabilities for truly human functioning.

But not everyone is likely to be convinced by this 'objectivist' reasoning. An apparently alternative way to interpret the 'dictates of nature' is to understand individuals' 'natures' as given by their 'identities'. We speak today of individual and collective *identities* – and thereby neatly express ambivalence over whether the nature of individuals and groups is objectively given or subjectively, and inter-subjectively, constructed. It has been well said that the very term is ambiguous, 'torn between "hard" and "soft" meanings, essentialist connotations and constructivist qualifiers' (Brubaker and Cooper: 2). Used by both protagonists and analysts of identity politics, the very meaning of 'identity' hovers between the interests of the former and the insights of the latter, between the ideas of what is given and what is created or constructed, between finding one's true self and creating it, between self-discovery and self-invention, between primordial identification and post-modernist self-fashioning. One may identify with one's ascribed identity or one may seek to ignore or reject it. Accordingly, domination in respect of identity can take several different forms. One is insufficient recognition – the non-recognition or mis-recognition of ethnic or cultural or religious or geographical identities, which the members of subordinate and minority groups in a society endorse and to which they cleave. Or else people can be seen, and so see themselves, as irredeemably defined by a fixed and unalterable inferior and dependent status and set of roles from which there is no exit. So, for example, Martha Nussbaum records a report of Indian widows as having 'internalized society's perception of them as daughters, mothers, wives and widows (their identity invariably defined in terms of their relationship to men)'.[6] In both types of case there is a failure of recognition: in the first of an identity that is claimed by the actors, in the second of one that is denied to them. The unrecognized can be seen as dominated because in both 'the people or society around them mirror back to them a confining or contemptible picture of themselves', thereby 'imprisoning' them 'in a false, distorted, and reduced mode of being'. As Charles Taylor elaborates, the

> projection of an inferior or demeaning image on another can actually distort and oppress, to the extent that the image is internalized. Not only contemporary feminism but also race relations and discussions of multiculturalism are undergirded by the premise that the withholding of recognition can be a form of oppression.   (Taylor 1992: 25, 35)

But there is no reason to think of 'identity' only in terms of group-related identity. Indeed, a significant contemporary form of identity domination consists in what we might call *excessive* or unwanted recognition, where individuals are, in various ways and for differing reasons, disinclined to identify with some group or category ascribed to them, but are pressured into conformity, public self-ascription ('coming out of the closet') and solidarity. In this way identifiers – the entrepreneurs and mobilizers of identity politics – can dominate all those whose attitudes to the group or category in question are less committed, or else ambiguous, indifferent or even hostile: the quasi-identifiers, semi-identifiers, non-identifiers, ex-identi-fiers, trans-identifiers, multi-identifiers and anti-identifiers.

Identity-related or what we can call recognitional domina-tion can take more complex forms still where the dominant group or nation, in control of the means of interpretation and communication, project their own experience and culture as the norm, rendering invisible the perspective of those they dom-inate, while simultaneously stereotyping them and marking them out as 'other'. In doing so, they employ a range of power mechanisms, as the black poet Aimé Césaire observed when he wrote, 'I am talking of millions of men who have been skilfully injected with fear, inferiority complexes, trepidation, servility, despair, abasement.' These words are quoted by Frantz Fanon at the very beginning of his first book, *Black Skin, White Masks*.[7] In this and his other works, Fanon explored the psychological, social and political dimensions of this form of domination and the intimate relations between language, personality, sexual relations and political experience in the context of the struggle for independence and the post-colonial experience in Algeria and elsewhere in Africa. Yet it is important, finally, to note that the injection will be only partially effective: that the dominated will never fully internalize ways of interpreting the world that devalue and stereotype them but rather experience what the black American political thinker W. E. B. Du Bois called a kind of 'double consciousness', namely:

this sense of always looking at one's self through the eyes of others, of measuring one's soul by the tape of a world that looks on in amused contempt and pity.[8]

I suggested above that interpreting the 'dictates of one's nature' as meaning the dictates of identity, however understood, is *apparently* an alternative to the objectivist interpretation in terms of 'human nature'. Is it a genuine alternative? Why, after all, do we think, if we do, that people's identities, however understood, require recognition? What is good about identity and what justifies its recognition? If the claim is that recognizing identity is a good, that it is normatively required, that must be because doing so satisfies some 'basic' or 'real' interest in such recognition, to be framed, perhaps, in terms of a central human functioning. Moreover, on what basis do we decide that recognition is 'insufficient' or 'excessive' – whether it be of those who claim it or of those who are denied it, and whether the identity be group-related or individualistic? And how is one to decide among competing demands for such recognition, other than by some criterion independent of claims made by the entrepreneurs and mobilizers of identity? Taylor writes that in its absence, people come to accept 'false', 'distorted' and 'reduced' conceptions of themselves, but all this presupposes an answer to the question: false, distorted and reduced as compared to *what*? There must be an implicit notion of what it is to live free of the humiliations indicated. So, for example, according to Sen, citing Adam Smith, one of the central human 'functionings' is 'being unashamed to appear in public' (Sen 1985: 15). In short, it is hard to see how the notion of identity-related or recognitional domination can do without presupposing a notion of real or objective interests, grounded in a theory of human nature.

I have sought here to sketch something of the range, and mutual incompatibility, of plausible answers to the question: how are we to conceive of domination rendering those subject to it less free to live according to the dictates of their nature and judgment? These answers need to be spelt out by elaborating in detail its mechanisms, including those on which Foucault has focused our attention, such as the inculcation and policing of conceptions of sexual and mental 'normality', of norms of fashion and myths of beauty, and also of gender roles and age categories, and of ideological boundaries, as for instance between what is private and what is public and between market and non-market modes of allocation, the countless forms and modes of oppressive stereotyping, the framing and spinning of information in the mass media and in political campaigns, and the like. Furthermore, it is important to understand that power in its more overt one- and two-dimensional forms has all kinds of three-dimensional effects. These are often misperceived as merely the effects of some impersonal process of 'cultural transmission'. Barrington Moore has eloquently exposed that error:

> The assumption of inertia, that social and cultural continuity does not require explanation, obliterates the fact that both have to be recreated anew in each generation, often with great pain and suffering. To maintain and transmit a value system, human beings are punched, bullied, sent to gaol, thrown into concentration camps, cajoled, bribed, made into heroes, encouraged to read newspapers, stood up against a wall and shot, and sometimes even taught sociology. To speak of cultural inertia is to overlook the concrete interests and privileges that are served by indoctrination, education, and the entire complicated process of transmitting culture from one generation to the next. (Moore 1967: 486)

In all these various ways, domination can induce and sustain internal constraints upon self-determination – ways of undermining and distorting people's confidence in and sense of self and of misleading and subverting their judgment as to how best to advance their interests.

There are, of course, also implausible answers to the question: how are we to conceive of domination rendering those subject to it less free to live according to the dictates of their nature and judgment? One is all too familiar from the history of communism: to call those dictates 'objective' or 'real interests' which are imputed, from the outside, by observers or activists, to individuals on the basis of their social location ('bourgeois', 'petty bourgeois', 'workers', etc.). But that is to view social actors as simply the bearers of social roles, identifying their interests with the requirements of their roles. The implausibility is compounded when their interests are taken to lie in reaching their assigned destinations or destinies within some grand narrative that is, in turn, assumed to be true. Various memorable kinds of Marxist – determinist, structuralist and vulgar – have taken this line (and it is not absent from the passages from Gramsci quoted in *PRV*), which leads them, when people fail to pursue or perceive their imputed interests, to explain, as Gyorgy Lukács did, this failure away as 'false consciousness.' But all that is an old story, to which we will return at the end of this chapter.

A second implausible answer is one we have encountered in our discussion of Foucault's treatment of power: that domination cannot make those subject to it any less (broadly) autonomous since there is no available state of being more autonomous. There is no escaping domination, for power is everywhere, precluding liberation and imposing regimes of truth. In his earlier writings on this topic, his suggestion was that both the nature and judgment of the 'subject' were fully 'constituted' by power relations and, as we have seen, innumerable Foucault-influenced writers have made suggestions such as that 'identity is itself the product of power relations' and that his arguments have undermined 'the model of the rational autonomous agent'. As we have also seen, Foucault came to disown this ultra-radical view, which would, in any case, both render resistance to domination unintelligible and undermine Foucault's own critical standpoint and political positions.

The upshot of the foregoing discussion is that the plausible answers to the question of how to interpret domination do not boil down to a single answer. Adherents of the minimal view of freedom can defensibly claim that domination just is subjecting populations or minorities or individuals to external coercions and constraints that restrict their options to live as they choose, but that they are to be viewed as autonomous and rational actors faced with feasible sets of choices, more or less aware of the external constraints they face, sometimes co-operating, even collaborating with those who dominate them, and resisting, even rebelling, when the opportunity arises. The other, non-minimal views here surveyed challenge and complicate this picture by raising the issue of *internal constraints* – of what is variously called 'the formation of preferences', 'internalization' and 'hegemony'. In other words, they address the ways in which domination can work against people's interests by stunting, diminishing and undermining their powers of judgment and by falsifying, distorting and reducing their self-perceptions and self-understanding. But, although they offer various, different defensible accounts of how this happens, they give divergent answers to what constitutes a rationally defensible and undistorted account of what those interests are (and how to arrive at it). And that is why I continue to maintain that the concept of power as domination is essentially contested.

Defending the Third Dimension

But, if this much is granted, the question then arises: how can any given account of domination and its mechanisms be shown to be superior to others? In particular, how is the three-dimensional view to be defended against its competitors? I can think of no better, indeed no other, way than to test its plausibility by seeing how it fares when confronted with alternative views, and, in particular, the most plausible of these. To this end, I shall consider the alternative view advanced in James Scott's impressive book *Domination and the Arts of Resistance: Hidden Transcripts* (Scott 1990; see also Scott 1985, chapter 8). Scott proposes a way of studying power relations, an 'interpretation of quiescence' and a 'critique of hegemony and false consciousness'.[9] His subtle analysis amounts to an explicit challenge to the sort of view advanced here and is supported by compelling evidence from a range of different societies and contexts.

That evidence is mostly drawn from 'studies of slavery, serfdom, untouchability, racial domination – including colonialism, and highly stratified peasant societies' and also from 'total institutions such as jails and prisoner of war camps' (Scott 1990: 20, x), and I shall later suggest reasons for thinking that such evidence may be predisposed to favour Scott's thesis. The thesis, in a nutshell, is that the victims of domination are to be seen as tactical and strategic actors, who dissemble in order to survive; as Tilly puts it, 'compliance, under Scott's microscope, turns out to be a sort of constant rebellion' (Tilly 1991: 598) or, to cite the Ethiopian proverb Scott uses as an epigraph to his book, 'When the great lord passes, the wise peasant bows deeply and silently farts.' He adduces evidence of two main kinds. On the one hand, there are the 'hidden transcripts' – generated in secluded settings, behind the scenes in the victims' 'life apart in the slave quarters, the village, the household, and in religious and ritual life', in 'a social space in which offstage dissent to the official transcript of power relations may be voiced', in forms such as 'linguistic disguises, ritual codes, taverns, fairs, the "hush arbors" of slave religion' and consisting in 'hopes of a returning prophet, ritual aggression via witchcraft, celebration of bandit heroes and resistance martyrs' (pp. 85, xi). On the other hand, there are the open but disguised expressions of ideological insubordination that can be decoded by interpreting 'the rumors, gossip, folktales, songs, gestures, jokes and theater of the powerless as vehicles by which, among other things, they insinuate a critique of power while hiding behind anonymity or behind innocuous understandings of their conduct' (p. xiii).

By contrast, the 'official' or 'public transcript' (which constitutes most of the evidence to which historians and social scientists have access) tells a quite different story. It will, Scott writes, 'provide convincing evidence for the hegemony of dominant values, for the hegemony of dominant discourse'. Here is where

the effects of power relations are most manifest, and any analysis based exclusively on the public transcript is likely to conclude that subordinate groups endorse the terms of their subordination and are willing, even enthusiastic, partners in that subordination. (p. 4)

On the open stage, 'the serfs or slaves will appear complicitous in creating an appearance of consent and unanimity; the show of discursive affirmations from below will make it seem as if ideological hegemony were secure'. Indeed, the power of the dominant ... ordinarily elicits – in the public transcript – a continuous stream of performances of deference, respect, reverence, admiration, esteem, and even adoration that serve further to convince ruling elites that their claims are in fact validated by the social evidence they see before their very eyes. (pp. 87, 93)

Thus, he argues, it is no surprise that so many have accepted the idea of a dominant or hegemonic ideology which, while not entirely excluding the interests of subordinate groups, 'operates to conceal or misrepresent aspects of social relations that, if apprehended directly, would be damaging to the interests of dominant elites'. He proposes that there is a thick and a thin version of such 'false consciousness':

The thick version claims that a dominant ideology works its magic by persuading subordinate groups to believe actively in the values that explain and justify their own subordination. . . . The thin theory of false consciousness, on the other hand, maintains only that the dominant ideology achieves compliance by convincing subordinate groups that the social order in which they live is natural and inevitable. The thick theory claims consent; the thin theory settles for resignation. (p. 72)[10]

Indeed, Scott notices, the idea of ideological incorporation, which he is concerned to contest, extends further into mainstream social science, in the form of Parsonian sociology, which assumes that subordinate social groups come 'naturally to an acceptance of the normative principles behind the social order without which no society could endure'. Such theories, he argues, owe their seductiveness in large part to 'the strategic appearances that elites and subordinates alike ordinarily insert into the public transcript'; unless 'one can penetrate the official transcript of both subordinates and elites, a reading of the social evidence will almost always represent a confirmation of the status quo in hegemonic terms' (pp. 86, 89, 90).

What, then, is the real story according to Scott? It is a story of near-universal dissimulation and resistance under external constraints. In ordinary circumstances,

> subordinates have a vested interest in avoiding any *explicit* display of insubordination. They also, of course, always have a practical interest in resistance – in minimizing the exactions, labor and humiliations to which they are subject. The reconciliation of these two objectives that seem at cross-purposes is typically achieved by pursuing precisely those forms of resistance that avoid any open confrontation with the structures of authority being resisted. Thus the peasantry, in the interests of safety and success, has historically preferred to disguise its resistance.   (p. 86)

It is a story of rational calculation: with 'rare, but significant exceptions, the public performance of the subordinate will, out of prudence, fear, and the desire to curry favor, be shaped to appeal to the expectations of the powerful'. And it is a story of interaction between rational actors where, although the actual balance of forces is never precisely known, there is a 'constant testing of the equilibrium' in a 'process of search and probing' where there is a 'structure of surveillance, reward and punishment' and a 'basic antagonism of goals between dominant and subordinates that is held in check by relations of discipline and punishment'(pp. 4, 192–3). The 'dominant elite . . . is ceaselessly working to maintain and extend its material control and symbolic reach' and the subordinate group is 'correspondingly devising strategies to thwart and reverse that appropriation and to take symbolic liberties as well' (p. 197).

Scott claims that this is true of 'slavery, serfdom, caste domination' and in 'those peasant–landlord relations in which appropriation and status degradation are joined'; it may, he adds, be applicable to 'certain institutional settings between wardens and prisoners, staff and mental patients, teachers and students, bosses and workers'. But these last two examples raise the issue of the *scope* of Scott's analysis. Sometimes he suggests that it is generalizable beyond the range of the systematically repressive societies and contexts originally indicated. Thus he writes that his confidence in making his case is 'bolstered by studies of working-class values in liberal democracies' (p. 112), and he clearly sees his argument as relevant to the question of how to interpret conforming behaviour by the less powerful where 'there is no apparent use of coercion (for example, violence, threats) to explain that conformity' (p. 71).

Scott's case actually takes two different forms, which need to be distinguished from one another. One is an empirical thesis, covering the range of societies and contexts originally indicated. Thus he writes that evidence against the

> thick theory of mystification is pervasive enough to convince me that it is generally untenable – particularly so for systems of domination such as serfdom, slavery and untouchability, in which consent and civil rights hardly figure even at the rhetorical level. (p. 72)

And he argues that this also holds for the thin theory, according to which ideological domination defines for subordinate groups 'what is realistic and what is not realistic' and drives 'certain aspirations and grievances into the realm of the impossible, of idle dreams' (p. 74). In short, on the historical evidence, 'little or no basis exists for crediting either a fat theory or a thin theory of hegemony':

> The obstacles to resistance, which are many, are simply not attributable to the inability of a subordinate to *imagine* a counterfactual social order. They do imagine both the reversal and negation of their domination, and, most important, they have acted on these values in desperation and on those rare occasions when the circumstances allowed. ... And having imagined a counterfactual social order, subordinate groups do not appear to have been paralyzed by an elite-fostered discourse intended to convince them that their efforts to change

their situation are hopeless ... since slave and peasant upris-
ings occur frequently enough and fail almost invariably, one
can make a persuasive case that whatever misperception of
reality prevails was apparently one that was more hopeful
than the facts warranted.   (pp. 81–2)

The other version of Scott's case is the general principle he follows in his interpretation of quiescence, which enjoins that,
when confronted with compliant behaviour and/or discourse of
subordinate groups, one should understand them in terms of tactics and strategy rather than consent or resignation. As Scott
himself observes, it is usually 'impossible to know from the
public transcript alone how much of the appeal to hegemonic
values is prudence and formula and how much is ethical submission' and 'exactly how deep [the] apparent acceptance of
the dominant discourse goes is ... impossible to judge from the
public evidence' (pp. 92, 103). In the absence of direct evidence
from behind the scenes, from the slave quarters or hush-arbors,
the available evidence is, of necessity, indirect and indeterminate (since Scott's other mode of access to the 'hidden transcripts' is further interpretation, decoding rumours, gossip and
so on). This raises the intriguing question of how we are to
decide which is the more plausible line of interpretation.

The problem with this interpretative strategy is that it begs
that question. It is true that Scott suggests an exception to its
applicability. Under 'limited and stringent conditions' that are
'not applicable to any of the large-scale forms of domination that
concern us here', he allows that what he calls a 'paper-thin
theory of hegemony' can apply. Subordinate groups may, he
concedes, 'come to accept, even legitimate, the arrangements
that justify their subordination' where there is a prospect of
upward mobility or escape from low status, or where there is
the 'total abolition of any social realm of relative discursive freedom', as in 'a few penal institutions, thought-reform camps, and
psychiatric wards' (pp. 82–5). Otherwise he just presumes that
his interpretative approach gives the right answer. That presumption is lent extra strength by the nature of the evidence to

which he directs it, drawn, as we have seen, from societies and contexts characterized by overt coercion, compulsory appropriation and systematic degradation, and 'free spaces' within which to develop subversive thoughts with others. One might suppose that consent and resignation are less likely where such coercion and oppression are more overt, and more likely where they are more covert and less severe. Scott evidently thinks so, for he remarks, '[c]oercion, it would seem, can produce compliance but it virtually inoculates the complier against willing compliance'; for 'the greater the external reasons compelling our action – here large threats and large rewards are comparable – the less we have to provide satisfactory reasons to ourselves for our conduct' (pp. 109, 110). This hypothesis is by no means obviously true, but it is why I suggested above that his evidence may be predisposed to favour his thesis.

But the question of how to interpret quiescence remains unanswered. Scott convincingly accounts for a wide range of evidence of 'the often fugitive political conduct of subordinate groups' where 'the powerless are often obliged to adopt a strategic pose in the presence of the powerful' and where 'the powerful may have an interest in overdramatizing their reputation and mastery' (p. xii). Furthermore, he several times cites *The Dominant Ideology Thesis* (Abercrombie et al. 1980), which effectively marshals the historical evidence against the thesis that subordinate classes were incorporated via ideological hegemony or integrated via common culture under feudalism, or under early and late capitalism.[11] He also cites Paul Willis's *Learning to Labour* (Willis 1977), which reveals the protective cynicism of English working-class schoolchildren. But neither he nor these other authors thereby succeed in showing that what I have called the third dimension of power is not also often and widely at work in shaping preferences, beliefs and desires and influencing judgment, in the range of societies and situations indicated. Indeed, when discussing John Gaventa's 'otherwise perceptive' study of the effects of third-dimensional power on Appalachian miners, *Power and Powerlessness: Quiescence and Rebellion in an Appalachian Valley* (Gaventa 1980), he concedes that both forms of power relation can co-exist. He remarks that Gaventa's book 'supports both a thick theory of false consciousness and a thin theory of naturalization' (p. 73) but also that his own account supplies 'the missing element in the theories of legitimation to be found' therein (p. 197). In societies and situations where coercion is less overt or absent, and inequalities more opaque, the question of how to interpret quiescence is all the more acute. What Scott has most effectively achieved is to provide a clearcut formulation and systematic exploration of just one way of answering it.

In short, there is no reason to view Scott's compelling account of the ingenious tactics and strategies of dissembling, ever-watchful slaves, peasants, untouchables and the like as *refuting* either the thick or the thin theory of hegemony. It does not show that there is not also widespread consent and resignation, in both pre-modern and modern societies, that is best explained by viewing these as both expressing and resulting from relations of power. The response of the wise Ethiopian peasant, who bows deeply to the great lord and silently farts, is, after all, only one among many. (What about all the unwise peasants?). Scott's approach is oddly monolithic: he makes no allowance for the compartmentalization of ideas and just takes it for granted that the dominated are, in George Eliot's phrase, 'acting a mask' of ostensibly compliant behaviour. Thus he considers, only to dismiss it, the 'alternative claim' that 'those obliged by domination to act a mask will eventually find that their faces have grown to fit the mask':

> The practice of subordination in this case produces, in time, its own legitimacy, rather like Pascal's injunction to those who were without religious faith but who desired it to get down on their knees five times a day to pray, and the acting would in the end engender its own justification in faith. (p. 10)

But why must we suppose these to be alternatives? As Farber comments, Scott 'does not explore the notion that these "alternatives" do not necessarily succeed each other in time but may exist side-by-side among the same groups and individuals' (Farber 2000: 103).

Indeed, once one begins to reflect on the matter, the alternatives of 'consent' and 'resignation' look like a hopelessly impoverished schema for describing and explaining the gamut of the remaining human responses to conditions of powerlessness and dependence, or the range of forms these conditions can take. Neither term adequately captures the range of cosmological, religious, moral and political ideas and everyday commonsensical assumptions whose acceptance has served to make such conditions appear intelligible and tolerable, or less intolerable, or indeed desirable.

Thus Nietzsche's slaves offer a sharp contrast to Scott's slaves, in their response to their condition. For Nietzsche, as for Scott, the slaves were self-interested and calculative. Indeed, they exhibited 'this basic prudence which even the insects have' that 'has tricked itself out in the garb of quiet, virtuous resignation, thanks to the duplicity of impotence – as though the weakness of the weak ... were a spontaneous act, a meritorious deed' (Nietzsche 1956[1887], I, 13). But for Nietzsche this took the creative form of a 'will to power' which found expression in the 'attempt to make those value judgments prevail that are favourable to *them*' (Nietzsche 1968[1906]: 400), so that they 'praise selflessness because it brings [them] advantages' (Nietzsche 1974[1882, 1887]: 21) – for 'every animal ... strives instinctively for the optimum conditions under which it may release its powers' (Nietzsche 1956[1887], III, 7). Nietzsche's 'genealogy of morals' is the story of the eventually victorious slaves' revolt in morality, in the Roman Empire between the first and third centuries AD, which created a new morality (that has since become indistinguishable from morality as such, so that its nature and origins have become invisible to us), a revaluation of values, attaching a positive valuation to a range of related practices and attitudes – notably, altruism, pity, Kantian respect for persons and egalitarianism, and revolving around the distinction between 'good' and 'evil'. So, for example, the slaves' impotence became 'goodness of heart', their anxious lowliness became 'humility', their 'inoffensiveness' and 'lingering at the door' became 'patience', the desire for retaliation became a desire for justice, and their hatred of the enemy a hatred of injustice (see Leiter 2002: 125). The triumph of slave morality and its associated 'ascetic ideal' – the morality associated with Christianity – was brought about through what Nietzsche called the '*ressentiment*' felt by the oppressed against their oppressors. Nietzsche writes of hearing

> the oppressed, downtrodden, violated whispering among themselves with the wily vengefulness of the impotent, 'Let us be unlike those evil ones. Let us be good. And the good shall be he who does not do violence, does not attack or retaliate, who leaves vengeance to God, who, like us, lives hidden, who shuns all that is evil, and altogether asks very little of life – like us, the patient, the humble, the just ones.' (Nietzsche 1956[1887], I, 13)

And they achieve their long-term victory under the influence and with the aid of 'the teachers, the leaders of humanity, theologians all of them' – 'that parasitical type of man – that of the priest – which has used morality to raise itself mendaciously to the position of determining human values – finding in Christianity the means to come to *power*' (Nietzsche 1967[1908], IV, 7).

Of course, Nietzsche's genealogy is a stylized historical narrative of polemical intent: it aims at nothing less than a critique of morality by seeking to bring 'a *feeling* of diminution in value of the thing that originated thus and prepares the way to a critical mood and attitude towards it' (Nietzsche 1968[1906]: 254). It is not a set of empirical claims based on comparative ethnographic research. But, first, as we have suggested, Scott's argument is not free of polemic and, second, Nietzsche's alternative interpretation of slave morality, whatever one may think of its plausibility, does direct us to the rich and suggestive field of religious teachings, viewed as interpretations of and responses to powerlessness and dependency. And, plainly, from the Sermon on the Mount to the Koran's pronouncements on the treatment and proper role of women to the Hindu *Laws of Manu*, such teachings have much to say that endorses active 'consent' to power by supplying justifying reasons for willing compliance and submissiveness (and some religious traditions, of course, have much to say that, in the name of humane values and equality among human beings, justifies neither[12]). Most of the world religions began with an egalitarian ethos, but they have interpreted and applied it selectively, above all in relation to women. As for 'resignation', the world's religions are also not lacking in messages that teach acquiescence in the 'natural' order of things, from Hindu world-renunciation to Buddhist character-planning, while translating (as Feuerbach taught Marx) human aspirations and dreams into supernatural fantasies (just as they can also, as Weber argued, inspire this-worldly activity and sometimes world-trans-forming activism).

Adaptive Preferences

What concerns us here, whether or not it is religiously induced or encouraged, is the shaping of agents' desires and beliefs by fac-tors external to those agents. Jon Elster has called this 'adaptive preference formation' – the trimming of desires to circum-stances. Of course, as several critics have pointed out, adjusting one's aspirations to what is feasible is sensible and indeed wise. What Elster is seeking to identify are those cases where the adap-tation is *non-autonomous*. What are the mechanisms of such adap-tation and how do they relate to three-dimensional power? *How*, in short, are such preferences in such cases formed?

Elster has given a very narrow interpretation of what is involved and he has sought to distinguish it sharply from the effects of power. He focuses on what he calls the mechanism of 'sour grapes', where people become content with what they can get, which he sees as one way of reducing cognitive dissonance. Referring to the fable of the fox and the grapes, in which the fox, unable to reach them, declares them sour, he gives 'adaptation' what he calls a 'causal' rather than an 'intentional' reading, and he takes this to be 'a strictly endogenous causality' (Elster 1983: 116). It is a trick our minds play on us, a 'purely causal process ... taking place "behind the back" of the person concerned', as opposed to 'the intentional shaping of desires' by the agent himself, as advocated, for example by Stoic, Buddhist and Spinozistic philosophies (p. 117). So he seeks to distinguish adaptive preferences from changes in desire that result from learning and experience and from preferences that result from 'precommitment' (deliberately excluding possible choices), character planning, and the like. These can all exemplify what Elster calls 'autonomous wants', where people are 'in control over the processes whereby their desires are formed, or at least ... not in the grip of processes with which they do not identify themselves' (p. 21), whereas adaptive preferences are 'shaped by the lack of alternatives' (p. 120), and result from a shift in desires supposedly caused by 'habituation and resignation' (p. 113), a nondeliberate adjustment of desire to the limits of what is seen to be feasible. But he also seeks to show that such adjustment to circumstances cannot result from the exercise of power, or that it is 'implausible' to suppose that it does (p. 116). His argument is not, however, convincing.

Elster takes issue with the following passage from *Power: A Radical View*:

A may exercise power over *B* by getting him to do what he does not want to do, but he also exercises power over him by influencing, shaping or determining his very wants. Indeed, is it not the supreme exercise of power to get another or others to have the desires you want them to have – that is, to secure their compliance by controlling their thoughts and desires? One does not have to go to the lengths of talking about *Brave New World*, or the world of B. F. Skinner, to see this: thought control takes many less total and more mundane forms, through the control of information, through the mass media, and through the processes of socialization.

The passage is, he (rightly) claims, ambiguous. Does it, he asks, 'propose a purposive or a functional explanation of wants?' If it means the latter, we have an instance of backward deduction from observed consequences, which is illegitimate unless a feedback mechanism can be specified that explains what is alleged to cause them: it may be 'good for the rulers that the subjects are resigned to their situation', but we need to know how this comes about. As for the former meaning, Elster asks: 'Do the rulers really have power to induce deliberately certain beliefs and desires in their subjects?' He asserts that such an explanation is 'implausible since the states in question are essentially by-products' – that is, 'mental and social states' that 'can never ... be brought about intelligently or intentionally, because the very attempt to do so precludes the state one is trying to bring about'.

But this last assertion is in serious need of justification. It is, in the first place, very far from obvious that the states of mind in question – desires and beliefs that endorse and even celebrate conforming to norms that are against one's interests or that express resignation to one's fate – are 'essentially by-products', inherently incapable of being deliberately inculcated. Unlike Elster, I cannot see why such outcomes cannot be the outcome of 'manipulation', though, of course, I agree that one must have evidence for such a claim: one should not be led into simply 'assuming that resignation generally is induced by those who benefit from it' (p. 115). But, second, as I have repeatedly insisted, to focus on 'manipulation' by defining the concept of power as deliberate intervention is unduly to narrow its scope. Power can be at work, inducing compliance by influencing desires and beliefs, without being 'intelligent and intentional'. And, third, there may indeed be a case for the functional interpretation of the passage cited, for there may be feedback mechanisms at work, which encourage 'subjects' to benefit 'rulers'.

Elster, over-impressed by the intriguing thought that power is impotent to bring about states that 'resist any attempt to bring them about deliberately' (p. 86), fails, for these reasons, to show that 'adaptive preferences' cannot be (or are not plausibly) induced and encouraged by power. And indeed there are well-known alternative interpretations of this phenomenon, which imply that they can and, indeed, often are. So Amartya Sen writes that the 'most blatant forms of inequalities and exploitations survive in the world through making allies out of the deprived and the exploited', as the

> underdog learns to bear the burden so well that he or she overlooks the burden itself. Discontent is replaced by acceptance, hopeless rebellion by conformist quiet, and ... suffering and anger by cheerful endurance.   (Sen 1984: 308–9)

He illustrates the point with a telling example. In 1944, the year after the Great Bengal Famine, a survey carried out by the All-India Institute of Hygiene and Public Health indicated a striking difference between the self-reports of widows and widowers in respect of their health. Though women were (and are) significantly more deprived with regard to health and nutrition, only 2.5% declared that they were 'ill' or in 'indifferent' health, as against 48.5% of the widowers. Asked the more specific and subjective question of whether they were in 'indifferent' health, 45.6% of the widowers declared that they were, as against *none* of the widows. Sen comments that

> Quiet acceptance of deprivation and bad fate affects the scale of dissatisfaction generated, and the utilitarian calculus gives sanctity to that distortion.   (Sen 1984: 309)[13]

Martha Nussbaum, who also cites this example, adds others concerning individual Indian women, in 'particular caste and regional circumstances', who are 'profoundly dependent on males' (Nussbaum 2000: 21): one, subjected to domestic violence from an alcoholic and spendthrift husband, lacked any sense of being wronged; another, with 'more deeply adaptive' preferences (p. 140), regarded her heavy labour at a brick kiln where women were never promoted or permitted to learn skills available to men, as natural and normal. As Nussbaum observes, such responses are the outcome of 'lifelong socialization and absence of information' (p. 139). But this last phrase needs to be unpacked, if it is to reveal the workings of power.

One thinker (also cited by Nussbaum) who tried to do so and was quite clear that power was at work in shaping and sustaining such adaptive preferences was John Stuart Mill. In his book *The Subjection of Women* (1989[1869]) he gives a remarkable account of the lifelong socialization of Victorian women, who formed, according to Mill, 'a subject-class . . . in a chronic state of bribery and intimidation combined' (p. 174). Men, he wrote,

> do not want solely the obedience of women, they want their sentiments. All men, except the most brutish, desire to have, in the woman most nearly connected with them, not a forced slave but a willing one, not a slave merely, but a favourite. They have therefore put everything in practice to enslave their minds. The masters of all other slaves rely, for maintaining obedience, on fear; either fear of themselves, or religious fears. The masters of women wanted more than simple obedience, and they turned the whole force of education to effect their purpose. All women are brought up from the very earliest years in the belief that their ideal of character is the very opposite of men; not self-will, and government by self-control, but submission, and yielding to the control of others. All the moralities tell them that it is the duty of women, and all the current sentimentalities that it is their nature, to live for others; to make complete abnegation of themselves, and to have no life but in their affections.

On Mill's account, the subjection of women consisted in a combination of external and internal – and internalized – constraints:

> When we put together three things – first, the natural attraction between opposite sexes; secondly, the wife's entire dependence on the husband, every privilege or pleasure she has being either his gift, or depending entirely on his will; and lastly, that the principal object of human pursuit, consideration, and all objects of social ambition, can in general be sought or obtained by her only through him, it would be a

miracle if the object of being attractive to men had not become the polar star of feminine education and formation of character. And, this great means of influence over the minds of women having been acquired, an instinct of selfishness made men avail themselves of it to the utmost as a means of holding women in subjection, by representing to them meekness, submissiveness, and resignation of all individual will into the hands of a man, as an essential part of sexual attractiveness. (pp. 26–9)[14]

Since Mill there have, of course, been many attempts to open up the 'black box' of what Mill here calls 'the formation of character' and others have come to call 'socialization', 'internalization' and 'incorporation', in ways that promise to illuminate the mechanisms of domination. Too often, however, these terms conceal an absence of explanation, suggesting cultural forces somehow impinging on individuals who somehow introject them (see Boudon 1998). What we need to know is how.

One such attempt is central to the work of Pierre Bourdieu. Addressing the same topic as Mill, Bourdieu's *Masculine Domination* formulates it thus:

> The dominated apply categories constructed from the point of view of the dominant to the relations of domination, thus making them appear as natural. This can lead to a kind of systematic self-depreciation, even self-denigration, visible in particular ... in the representation that Kabyle women have of their genitals as something deficient, ugly, even repulsive (or, in modern societies, in the vision that many women have of their bodies as not conforming to the aesthetic canon imposed by fashion), and, more generally, in their adherence to a demeaning image of woman. (Bourdieu 2001[1998]: 35)

Bourdieu argues that 'the only way to understand this particular form of domination is to move beyond the forced choice between constraint (by forces) and consent (to reasons), between mechanical coercion and voluntary, free, deliberate, even calculated submission' (p. 37).[15]

Bourdieu's proposed way forward is through the notion of what he rhetorically calls 'symbolic violence' – 'a gentle violence, imperceptible and invisible even to its victims' (pp. 1–2). 'The effect of symbolic domination (whether ethnic, gender, cultural or linguistic, etc.)' is to shape what Bourdieu calls '*habitus*', the embodied dispositions which yield 'practical sense'and organize actors' visions of the world below the level of consciousness in a way that is resistant to articulation, critical reflection and conscious manipulation. Such domination (p. 37) is

> exerted not in the pure logic of knowing consciousness but through the schemes of perception, appreciation and action that are constitutive of habitus and which, below the level of the decisions of consciousness and the controls of the will, set up a cognitive relationship that is profoundly obscure to itself.

Bourdieu comments on the 'paradoxical logic of masculine domination and feminine submissiveness, which can, without contradiction, be described as both *spontaneous* and *extorted*'. This cannot be understood, he claims, 'until one takes account of the *durable effects* that the social order exerts on women (and men), that is to say, the disposition spontaneously attuned to that order which it imposes on them'. On Bourdieu's account, symbolic force is

> a form of power that is exerted on bodies, directly and as if by magic, without any physical constraint, but this magic works only on the basis of the dispositions deposited, like springs, at the deepest level of the body ... it does no more than trigger the dispositions that the work of inculcation and embodiment has deposited in those who are thereby primed for it.

An 'immense preliminary labour' is needed 'to bring about a durable transformation of bodies and to produce the permanent dispositions that it triggers and awakens' and this 'transformative action is all the more powerful because it is for the most part exerted invisibly and insidiously through insensible familiarization with a symbolically structured physical world and early, prolonged experience of interactions informed by the structures of domination' (pp. 37–8).

Bourdieu's idea of domination through symbolic violence is that 'the effect and conditions of its efficacy are durably and deeply embedded in the body in the form of dispositions' (p. 39), generating practices adjusted to the various 'fields'. 'Fields', in Bourdieu's parlance, are stratified social spaces within which individuals struggle for unequally distributed resources or 'capital' (whether economic or cultural or symbolic, etc.). Social agents are 'endowed with habitus, inscribed in their bodies by past experience': social norms and conventions of the various fields are 'incorporated', or 'inscribed', into their bodies, thereby generating 'a permanent disposition, a durable way of standing, speaking, walking, and thereby of feeling and thinking' (Bourdieu 1990[1980]: 70). The dispositions that constitute habitus are 'spontaneously attuned' to the social order, perceived as self-evident and natural (Bourdieu 2000[1997]: 138–9). As applied to gender, he claims, the 'essential part of the learning of masculinity and femininity tends to inscribe the difference between the sexes in bodies (especially through clothing), in the form of ways of walking, talking, standing, looking, sitting, etc.' (ibid., p. 141).[16]

Bourdieu's abundant ethnographic studies of various 'fields' of social life are richly illustrative of aspects of power as domination that I have sought to emphasize: above all, the ways in which its effectiveness is enhanced by being disguised or rendered invisible, by 'naturalization', where what is conventional and position- or class-based appears to the actors as natural and objective, and by 'misrecognition' of its sources and modes of operation. Moreover, on Bourdieu's account, none of this is intentionally achieved: 'legitimation of the social world is not, as some believe, the product of a deliberate and purposive action of propaganda or symbolic imposition' (Bourdieu 1989 [1987]: 21). So, for example, gift-giving in Kabyle society is a way of binding others in the guise of generosity. 'Symbolic capital', such as educational credentials, gives those who hold it the power 'to impose the scale of values most favourable to their products – notably because in our societies, they hold a practical *de facto* monopoly over institutions which, like the school system, officially determine and guarantee rank'. So, for example, 'professors construct an image of their students, of their performance and of their value, and (re)produce, through practices of co-optation guided by the same categories, the very group of their colleagues and the faculty' (Bourdieu 1989[1987]: 21, 14). And in his study *Distinction* he describes in wonderful, novelistic detail the ways in which, in areas such as art, sports, newspaper reading, interior decoration, food consumption, linguistic habits, bodily aesthetic and so on, status distinctions are maintained and reinforced, as people classify themselves and expose themselves to classification. The class struggle becomes, in Bourdieu's hands, 'the classification struggle', in which what is at stake is 'power over the classificatory schemes and systems which are the basis of the representations of the groups and therefore of their mobilization and demobilization'. All of this occurs, according to Bourdieu, 'even without any conscious intention of distinction or explicit pursuit of difference' and as the result of 'strategies – which may be perfectly unconscious, and thereby even more effective' (Bourdieu 1984[1979]: 479, 246, 255). But, as Elster has observed, this appeal to 'unconscious strategies' is suspect as an explanatory device (Elster 1981),[17] and it is no more explanatory to be told that the 'objective differentiation of conditions and dispositions' produces 'automatic, unconscious effects' (Bourdieu 1984[1979]: 246).

All of which leads me to ask whether Bourdieu's theory of dispositional practices, inscribed in bodies and spontaneously attuned to the conditions of existence of social positions, promises to open the black box of domination through incorporation. Does it help to explain the 'magic' (Bourdieu also likes to speak of the 'alchemy') of 'power exerted on bodies'? The topic of the interplay between society and the physical, chemical and physiological functioning of the body, and in general the interpenetration of the social and the biological, is a fascinating one, about which we as yet understand very little.[18] Bourdieu's theorizing about it proposes a pre-discursive 'inscription of social structure into bodies'. The question is: is this proposal anything more than a suggestive metaphor and, if not, is the metaphor helpful in directing us towards explanations?[19] It certainly opens up an intriguing and important area for empirical investigation. But even if much (how much?) of learning, especially early learning, is physically and behaviourally 'embodied', what exactly does this explain? There are convincing and well-studied cases, in both pre-modern and modern settings, of 'bodily knowledge' reflecting and reproducing hierarchies of social positions with 'fields' (see, for instance, Wacquant 2003), but how far can they be generalized? Where, when and how does tacit, practical embodied knowledge set limits to 'discursive' learning and self-transformation? Our ways of speaking doubtless indicate and reinforce our social positions in ways that probably go deep, and it is both plausible and illuminating to see social significance in the ways people view, use and treat their bodies, as 'body language', for instance, expressing and perpetuating class, gender and indeed national identities. But these can also be understood as responses to a whole array of 'discursive' cultural influences, from early socialization to religious teachings and the mass media, that are in turn subject to political influence and to historical changes. (So, for instance, it is likely that, after decades of feminism, there will have been changes in how young women view, hold and use their bodies, in sport, say, or during pregnancy.)

Bourdieu criticizes 'the whole Marxist tradition' and 'the feminist theorists who, giving way to habits of thought, expect political liberation to come from the "raising of consciousness"' on the ground that they ignore 'the extraordinary inertia which results from the inscription of social structure in bodies' (Bourdieu 2000[1997]: 172). But 'extraordinary inertia' goes far beyond what we currently know about the mechanisms and effects of bodily 'incorporation' and, moreover, appears to express a generalized view of 'internalization' beyond reflexive critique that is, in any case, hard to reconcile with Bourdieu's own activist and engaged politics. As for Marxism and feminism, what is clear is that they have opened up for investigation the very topic before us of the third dimension of power: the capacity to secure compliance to domination through the shaping of beliefs and desires, by imposing internal constraints under historically changing circumstances.

'Real Interests' and 'False Consciousness'

When, we must finally ask, does such shaping and imposition constitute domination? After all, enculturation is the source of much that we take to be true, right and good, and our reflective beliefs and desires presuppose and derive from countless others that we simply take for granted. What can make the securing of compliance through the acquisition of beliefs and the formation of preferences count as exemplifying 'domination'?

Marxists have not been over-helpful in confronting this question, since they have assumed its answer to be self-evident. Power is, at root, class power: the 'dominant ideology thesis' (in its most as in its least sophisticated versions) leaves no room for doubt that those subject to ideological domination are deflected from the perception and pursuit of their own class interests by hegemonic forms of thought. So, as indicated in Chapter 1, Gramsci thought that 'submission and intellectual subordination' could impede a subordinate class from following its 'own conception of the world'. Gramsci viewed civil society in the West as the site where consent is engineered, ensuring the cultural ascendancy of the ruling class and capitalism's stability. As Perry Anderson has expressed it, 'hegemony' for Gramsci, in this usage of the term, meant 'the ideological subordination of the working class by the bourgeoisie, which enables it to rule by consent' (Anderson 1976–7: 26). The subordinate classes under capitalism have, Gramsci thought, a dual and contradictory consciousness: they are split between the consciousness imposed on them and 'commonsense', which is 'fragmentary, incoherent and inconsequential, in conformity with the social and cultural position of those masses whose philosophy it is'. This latter expresses the worker's interests: it is 'implicit in his activity and ... in reality unites him with all his fellow-workers in the practical transformation of the real world', but it is immobilized by the dominant ideology, which is 'superficially explicit or verbal' and which 'he has inherited from the past and uncritically absorbed'. Gramsci assumed that ideological and political struggle would bring workers to see and pursue their 'real interests', whereas Gyorgy Lukács accounted (in a more Leninist mode) for their repeated failure to do so as 'false consciousness' with respect to the 'appropriate and rational reactions imputed to a particular typical position in the process of production'. This latter (true) consciousness 'imputed' to the class is 'neither the sum nor the average of what is thought or felt by the single individuals who make up the class' and yet 'the historically significant actions of the class are determined in the last resort by this consciousness' (Lukács 1971[1923]: 229).

But, of course, social actors do not have unitary or dual, but multiple and conflicting interests, which are interests of different kinds,[20] and their identities are not confined to their imputed class positions and destinies. And yet the Marxist account captures the remarkable capacity of ideological power to transform and subvert commonsense and practical experience, for, as Spinoza. remarked, a 'man's judgment may be influenced in many ways, some of them hardly credible'. The fundamental problem with the Marxist answer to the question, and with the language expressing it, appears to be with what lies behind it: namely, the claim to have some sort of privileged access, external to the actors, to a 'true' account of what is 'real' and of what are 'appropriate' and 'rational' responses to subordination. 'False consciousness' sounds patronizing, and 'real interests', if they conflict with material or subjectively avowed interests, sound presumptuous – and, indeed, without Marxist assumptions seem to lack any basis – which is why *PRV*'s first published critic accused it of 'employing a Marxian notion in a very non-Marxist way' (Bradshaw 1976 in Scott (ed.) 1994: 271).

But what exactly is the problem here? Is it the *content* of the Marxist analysis: in particular, the indicated exclusionary focus on class? Or is it the self-assurance and often dogmatism with which Marxist thinkers, sectarians and party secretaries across the decades have been ready to attribute 'real interests' and 'false consciousness' to others? Or is it, thirdly, the very idea that in attributing power to some over others, and analysing its mechanisms, one may take a view that is external to those allegedly subject to it.

The first two possibilities constitute legitimate grounds for familiar and justified criticism, but the third does not. For the claim that compliance to domination can be secured by the shaping of beliefs and desires must invoke cognitive and evaluative judgments that are distinct from the relevant actual beliefs and desires of the actors alleged to be subject to it. In other words, the very idea of power's third dimension requires an external standpoint. Power as domination, I have argued, invokes the idea of constraint upon interests, and to speak of the third dimension of such power is to speak of interests imputed to and unrecognized by the actors. In *PRV* I suggested that there can be an 'empirical basis for identifying real interests', which is 'not up to *A*, *but to B* exercising choice under conditions of relative autonomy and, in particular, independently of *A*'s power – e.g. through democratic participation'. In support of this I might have cited cases such as the women's development groups in Andhra Pradesh in India referred to by Martha Nussbaum, among whose members '[t]raditions of deference that once seemed good have quickly ceased to seem so'. For, as Nussbaum writes, if

> someone who has no property rights under the law, who has no formal education, who has no legal right of divorce, who will very likely be beaten if she seeks employment outside the home, says that she endorses traditions of modesty, purity and self-abnegation, it is not clear that we should consider this the last word on the matter.

We should, in short, 'reflect before we conclude that women without options really endorse the lives they lead' (Nussbaum 2000: 43). But nor should we just assume that people *with* options do so, if those options are loaded and internal constraints work against their interests.

But how can we speak of 'real' interests, given that, as I have argued, people's interests are many, conflicting and of different kinds? For example, where is one's 'real' interest if one's 'well-being interest' (or 'strong evaluation' or 'meta-preference') conflicts with one's 'welfare interest' in meeting a basic need – as when fundamentalist Christian believers refuse life-saving medical interventions on the grounds that they violate God's will and will damn them eternally?[21] And how can the claim be defended that there is 'an empirical basis for identifying real interests' and that this is 'not up to *A*, *but to B,* exercising choice under conditions of relative autonomy'? For, as another early critic of *PRV* insisted,

> the judgment as to *which* class of wants, preferences, choices, etc. do constitute the interests of an actor who is subject to an exercise of power has to be made by the external observer, or analyst *on behalf of* the actor. The judgment that has to be made is how the actor would feel or behave under conditions which do not now hold, and maybe never have, nor ever will hold. No matter how well-intentioned the observer, this is still other-ascription of interests, and not self-ascription. (Benton 1981 in Scott (ed.) 1994: vol. 2, p. 288)

Moreover, there are problems in identifying empirically what counts as 'relative autonomy':

> If a temporary withdrawal of the exercise of *A*'s power over *B* is supposed, how do we know when enough of his power has been withdrawn for it to be legitimate to call *B*'s expressed preferences at that point expressions of his/hers/its 'real' interests? How do we know that *A* is not affected by an exercise of power from some third source, *C*? and so on?

And, further, why should these conditions be privileged for the purposes of interest-ascription: 'why are conditions of relative autonomy the ones which are chosen'? Once more it is 'the external observer who decides (through the choice of conception of interests) which among the indefinitely large class of counter-factual conditions are to be the privileged ones for purposes of interest-ascription'. And is this counterfactual reasoning even coherent? If 'we are to imagine the outcome of socializing practices which are radically reorganized and quite different from the ones with which we are familiar ... then it is hard to see how it would be appropriate to speak of the *same* actor as author of the hypothetical preferences, wants, etc.' (ibid., pp. 289–91). And, in being asked to entertain the requisite coun-terfactual, are we not brought 'ever closer to a ridiculously barren, asocial arena' (Bradshaw 1976 in Scott (ed.) 1994: vol. 2, p. 270)?

These difficulties become less serious if one simply takes what count as 'real interests' to be a function of one's explanatory pur-pose, framework and methods, which in turn have to be justified. There is no reason to believe that there exists a canonical set of such interests that will constitute 'the last word on the matter' – that will resolve moral conflicts and set the seal on proffered explanations, confirming them as true. So the evidence from Indian women's collectives is relevant and compelling, if one can show convincingly that there is no 'third source' of pressure upon their members. If one is advancing a 'materialist' explana-tion, like Przeworski's, of, say, class compromise under capital-ism, then 'real' interests will be material interests. If one is seeking to explain choice under constraints within a 'rational choice' framework, then 'real interests' can mean individuals' 'best interests', for 'in so far as the choice situations in which indi-viduals find themselves restrict the feasible set, they may be said to work against their wider interests' (Dowding 1991: 43). Thus if Crenson's steelworkers in Gary, Indiana, are forced to trade off air pollution against employment, their real or best interest is to render clean air and employment compatible, which would require pollution controls throughout the United States, so that no community is relatively disadvantaged by them. Or 'real interests' can be understood as a way of identifying 'basic' or 'central' capabilities which existing arrangements pre-clude. So, to cite Nussbaum once more, the seclusion of women in the north of India, who 'just peep out of their houses and don't take any action in the world' is 'incompatible with fully human functioning' (Nussbaum 2000: 43).[22]

What, finally, about attributions of 'false consciousness'. *PRV* has been repeatedly accused of employing this discredited notion. Lukes, one critic writes,

> resurrects the spectre of false consciousness which many had thought exorcized from contemporary social and political theory. The problem with such a formulation is the deeply condescending conception of the social subject as an ideological dupe that it conjures up. Not only is this wretched individual incapable of perceiving her/his true interests, pacified as s/he is by the hallucinogenic effects of bourgeois indoctrination. But rising above the ideological mists is the enlightened academic who from his/her perch in the ivory tower may look down to discern the genuine interests of those not similarly blessed.   (Hay 1997: 47–8)

'False consciousness' is an expression that carries a heavy weight of unwelcome historical baggage. But that weight can be removed if one understands it to refer, not to the arrogant assertion of a privileged access to *truths* presumed unavailable to others, but rather to a cognitive power of considerable significance and scope: namely, *the power to mislead*. It takes many forms, some of which we have considered – from straightforward censorship and disinformation to the various institutionalized and personal ways there are of infantilizing judgment, and the promotion and sustenance of all kinds of failures of rationality and illusory thinking, among them the 'naturalization' of what could be otherwise and the misrecognition of the sources of desire and belief. Is it plausible to doubt the reality, prevalence and significance of such power in the world in which we live – whatever we may conclude, after investigation, about its scope and effectiveness in particular situations? Moreover, to recognize its very possibility is not, as suggested by Hay and many others, to be loftily condescending. Nor is it inherently illiberal and paternalist, or a licence for tyranny. Reference to the power to secure willing consent to domination is, for instance, an essential part of John Stuart Mill's analysis of the subjection of women, though, as he himself rightly pointed out, there were increasingly many women who were clearly aware of it.[23]

False consciousness, thus construed, is always partial and limited. In his book *One-Dimensional Man*, Herbert Marcuse wrote that an increasingly all-embracing 'one-dimensional thought'

> is systematically promoted by the makers of politics and their purveyors of mass information. Their universe of discourse is populated by self-validating hypotheses which, incessantly and monopolistically repeated, become hypnotic definitions or dictations.   (Marcuse 1964: 14)

But three-dimensional power does not and cannot produce one-dimensional man. Power's third dimension is always focused on particular domains of experience and is never, except in fictional dystopias, more than partially effective. It would be simplistic to suppose that 'willing' and 'unwilling' compliance to domination are mutually exclusive: one can *consent* to power and *resent* the mode of its exercise.[24] Furthermore, internalized illusions are entirely compatible with a highly rational and clear-eyed approach to living with them. Susan Bordo gives a good illustration of this:

> Recognizing that normalizing cultural forms exist does not entail, as some writers have argued, the view that women are 'cultural dopes', blindly submitting to oppressive regimes of beauty. Although many people *are* mystified (insisting, for example, that the current fitness craze is only about health or that plastic surgery to 'correct' a 'Jewish' or 'black' nose is just an individual preference), often there will be a high degree of consciousness involved in the decision to diet or have cosmetic surgery. People *know* the routes to success in this culture − they are advertised widely enough − and they are not 'dopes' to pursue them. Often, given the sexism, racism, and

narcissism of the culture, their personal happiness and economic security may depend on it.   (Bordo 2003: 30)

And in general, as Foucault insisted, power meets resistance, for,
as Spinoza, once more, observed,

> in spite of all that political skill has been able to achieve in this
> field, it has never been completely successful; men have always
> found that individuals were full of their own ideas, and that
> opinions varied as much as tastes.

NOTES

Notes to the Introduction

1 The basis in Marx and Engels for Gramsci's idea is their claim that the 'ideas of the ruling class are in every epoch the ruling ideas: i.e., the class, which is the ruling *material* force of society, is at the same time its ruling *intellectual* force. The class which has the means of material production at its disposal, has control at the same time over the means of mental production, so that thereby, generally speaking, the ideas of those who lack the means of mental production are subject to it' (Marx and Engels 1965[1845]: 60). For discussions of Gramsci on hegemony, see Williams 1965 and Bates 1975.

2 On this point, Stephen Holmes has reminded me of Joseph Schumpeter's shrewd observation concerning Lincoln's dictum that you can't fool all the people all the time: that it is enough to fool them in the short run, since history 'consists of a succession of short-run situations that may alter the course of events for good' (Schumpeter 1962[1950]: 264).

3 It is hard to say which is the better interpretation. Gramsci's text resembles Wittgenstein's duck/rabbit (if you look at it one way, it is a duck; if you look at it another way, it is a rabbit) and this cannot be unconnected with the circumstances under which it was written.

4 Discussed at length below in Chapter 3.

Notes to Chapter 1   Power: A Radical View

1 Contrast Parsons's lament that 'Unfortunately, the concept of power is not a settled one in the social sciences, either in political science or in sociology' (Parsons 1957: 139).

2 For a critical discussion of Dahl's use of his own concept of power, see Morriss (1972).

Notes

3 Emphasis mine (S.L.) This passage is acutely criticised in Morriss 1972.

4 Another example occurs on pp. 161–2 and p. 321, when Dahl points implicitly towards the process of nondecision-making, by writing of the power of members of the political stratum partly to determine whether a matter becomes a 'salient public issue' or not.

5 Compare Theodor Geiger's critique of Marx's imputation of 'true interests' to the proletariat which are independent of the wishes and goals of its members: here, writes Geiger, 'the proper analysis of the interest structure of social classes ends – religious mania alone speaks here' (*Die Klassengesellschaft im Schmelzliegel*, Cologne and Hagen, 1949, p. 133 cited and translated in Dahrendorf 1959: 175).

6 On coercion see Nozick 1972; Pennock and Chapman (eds) 1972. See also Wertheimer 1987.

7 See Lukes 1973, chapter 17. Contrast Dahrendorf's decision to 'follow ... the useful and well-considered definitions of Max Weber', according to which 'the important difference between power and authority consists in the fact that whereas power is essentially tied to the personality of individuals, authority is always associated with social positions or roles' (Dahrendorf 1959: 166).

8 Karl Marx and Friedrich Engels, 'The Eighteenth Brumaire of Louis Bonaparte', in Marx and Engels 1962, vol. 1: 247.

9 This association is made most clearly in *Power and Poverty* (Bachrach and Baratz 1970: esp. pp. 49–50) in reaction to the pressure of pluralist criticisms of the (potentially three-dimensional) implications of the article on nondecisions (Bachrach and Baratz 1963). See Merelman (1968b) and Bachrach and Baratz 1968.

10 I use the term 'behavioural' in the narrow sense indicated above, to refer to the study of overt and actual behaviour – and specifically concrete decisions. Of course, in the widest sense, the three-dimensional view of power is 'behavioural' in that it is committed to the view that behaviour (action and inaction, conscious and unconscious, actual and potential) provides evidence (direct and indirect) for an attribution of the exercise of power.

11 This conflict is latent in the sense that it is assumed that there *would be* a conflict of wants or preferences between those exercising power and those subject to it, were the latter to become aware of their interests. (My account of latent conflict and real interests is to be distinguished from Dahrendorf's account of 'objective' and 'latent' interests as 'antagonistic interests conditioned by, even inherent in, social positions', in imperatively co-ordinated associations, which are 'independent of [the individual's] conscious orientations' (Dahrendorf 1959: 174, 178). Dahrendorf assumes as sociologically given what I claim to be empirically ascertainable.)

Notes

12 This distinction between 'concept' and 'view' is closely parallel to that drawn by John Rawls between 'concept' and 'conception'. It seems, writes Rawls,

> natural to think of the concept of justice as distinct from the various conceptions of justice and as being specified by the role which these different sets of principles, these different conceptions, have in common. Those who hold different conceptions of justice can, then, still agree that institutions are just when no arbitrary distinctions are made between persons in the assigning of basic rights and duties and when the rules determine a proper balance between competing claims to the advantages of social life. Men can agree to this description of just institutions since the notions of an arbitrary distinction and of a proper balance, which are included in the concept of justice, are left open for each to interpret according to the principles of justice that he accepts. These principles single out which similarities and differences among persons are relevant in determining rights and duties and they specify which division of advantages is appropriate. (Rawls 1972: 5–6).

Analogously, those holding the three different views of power I have set out offer differing interpretations of what are to count as interests and how they may be adversely affected. I further agree with Rawls's suggestions that the various conceptions of justice (like views of power) are 'the outgrowth of different notions of society against the background of opposing views of the natural necessities and opportunities of human life. Fully to understand a conception of justice we must make explicit the conception of social co-operation from which it derives' (pp. 9–10). I disagree, however, with Rawls's apparent belief that there is ultimately one rational conception or set of principles of justice to be discovered. 'Justice' is no less essentially contested than 'power'.

13 Thus for Parsons 'the power of A over B' becomes a 'right' of precedence in decision-making!

14 On this last point, see the writings of Peter Bachrach.

15 See Barry 1965, and the present author's discussion of it in Lukes 1967.

16 Cf. Connolly's 'first approximation' to a definition of real interests: 'Policy x is more in A's interest than policy y, if A were he to experience the *results* of both x and y, would *choose x* as the result he would rather have for himself' (Connolly 1972: 472). I too connect real interests with (relative) autonomy and choice. What is, of course, required at this point is a sustained discussion of the nature of, and conditions for, autonomy (and its relation to social determination). See Lukes 1973, chapters 8, 18 and 20.

17 On the other hand, Crenson's use of the reputational method for locating power does lead him to focus on the *motives* of industrialists, political leaders, etc. and thus to ignore 'the possibility of more impersonal,

154

structural and systematic explanations', such as that 'certain forms of city government in the United States are poorly adapted to handle this particular issue' of air pollution (Newton 1972: 487).

18   However, it should be noted that his statistical correlations are rather low (the highest being 0.61, and most being between 0.20 and 0.40). Strictly speaking, Crenson offers only highly plausible hypotheses which are not controverted by his evidence but only weakly suported by it.

19   Note Gramsci's reliance on the notion of autonomy here.

20   See, e.g., Somjee 1972. Somjee writes that in the village he studied, 'In the five successive panchayat elections, respect for age, cohesiveness of caste and kin-group, and familial status gradually declined. The elective principle, which was at the heart of the structural changes, had made serious inroads into the sociopolitical continuum of the traditional society. The all-pervading trends emanating from the old social organization and affecting the structure of community politics and its attitude to authority began to be reversed' (p. 604).

21   See Isaacs 1964, exp. chapter 12, 'Ways Out).

22   See Lewis (ed.) 1967, vol. viii: 428–9. When the Muslims conquered India's caste cities in the eleventh and twelfth centuries, the result was that 'the egalitarian principles of Islam attracted large numbers of non-caste Hindus and professional groups to the fold of Islam' (ibid.).

23   The most notable recent instance was the mass conversion of Untouchables to Buddhism under B. R. Ambedkhar's leadership in 1956. In a famous speech in 1936, Ambedkhar had said, 'My self-respect cannot assimilate Hinduism . . . I tell you, religion is for men, not men for religion . . . The religion that does not recognise you as human beings, or give you water to drink, or allow you to enter the temples is not worthy to be called a religion. . . .' (cited in Isaacs 1964: 173).

24   Though caste lines were, in fact, maintained within the social systems of the Christians and the Muslims (see Isaacs 1964: 171).

25   The first contributions of the Poulantzas–Miliband debate are reproduced in Urry and Wakeford (eds) 1973. It is discussed by Ernest Laclau in Laclan 1975 and continued by Poulantzas in (1976).

26   'Compare Wright Mills:

Fate is a feature of specific kinds of social structure; the extent to which the mechanics of fate are the mechanics of history-making is itself a historical problem. . . .

In those societies in which the means of power are involuntary and decentralized, history *is* fate. The innumerable actions of innumerable men modify their local milieus, and thus gradually modify the structure of society as a whole. These modifications – the course of history – go on behind men's backs. History is drift, although in total 'men make it'.

But in those societies in which the means of power are enormous in scope and centralized in form a few men may be so placed within the historical structure that by their decisions about the use of these means they modify the structural conditions under which most men live. Nowadays such elites of power make history, 'under circumstances not chosen altogether by themselves', yet compared with other men, and with other periods of human history, these circumstances do indeed seem less overwhelming.   (Mills 1959: 21–2)

27   On this, see William Connolly's discussion of power in Connolly 1983.
28   For a fine example of such an analysis, see Gaventa 1980.

Notes to Chapter 2   Power, Freedom and Reason

1   For this distinction see Bourdieu 1990[1980]), Chapter 5.
2   One response to this is 'scientific realism', which maintains that powers derive from the agent's intrinsic nature or constitution (Harré and Madden 1975). Another might be Jon Elster's: that law-like explanation in the social sciences is implausible and fragile, and that 'mechanisms' allow us to explain but not to predict (Elster 1998 and 1999: Chapter 1)
3   See Komter 1989. For instance, a wife's interests may align with her husband's but for different reasons. He make think she takes his clothes to the laundromat because she accepts that this is her job, but she may have quite different reasons: to socialize with her friends or maybe she is having an affair. (I owe this example to Suzanne Fry.)
4   I owe this example, though not this use of it, to Iris Marion Young.
5   Jon Elster has noticed that this fallacy was identified by Max Scheler as occurring when 'our factual inability to acquire a good is wrongly interpreted as a positive action against our desire' (Scheler 1972: 52 cited in Elster 1983: 70).
6   Compare Marx's formulation of this interplay: 'The silent compulsion of economic relations sets the seal on the domination of the capitalist over the worker. Direct extra-economic force is still of course used, but only in exceptional cases. In the ordinary run of things, the worker can be left to the natural laws of production, – i.e. it is possible to rely on his dependence on capital, which springs from the conditions of production themselves, and is guaranteed in perpetuity by them' (Marx 1976 [1867]: 899).
7   It has also led some feminists to think of power as a resource to be redistributed (e.g. Okin 1989) – a view that can be traced back to John Stuart Mill. Compare Iris Young's critique of the 'distributive paradigm' applied to power (Young 1990: 30–3) and Amy Allen's

156

observation that although 'the ability to exercise power may be enhanced by the possession of certain key resources (money, self-esteem, weapons, education, political influence, physical strength, social authority, and so on), this ability should not be conflated with those resources themselves' (Allen 1999: 10).

8   I say explicitly, since, in general, the outcomes resulting from social power will presuppose social relations.

9   Oddly, Morriss thinks that 'social and political power is usually a sort of ableness and not an ability' (Morriss 2002: 83).

10   This point was clear to Max Weber who, when he defines power as the chance of an actor or actors to realize their will, adds the clauses 'despite resistance' and, more tellingly, 'even against the resistance of others' (Weber 1978[1910–14]: 53, 926).

11   I take preferences to be structured, standing, rankable dispositions to choose certain states of affairs rather than others that in turn imply dispositions to act in one way rather than another under specified conditions.

12   Including the present writer in *PRV*.

13   A point noticed in the sixteenth century by La Boétie when he remarked that it is 'the inhabitants themselves who permit, or rather bring about, their own servitude' (Boétie 1998[1548]: 194). See Rosen 1996.

14   In his 'Answer to the Question: What is Enlightenment?', Kant wrote, '*Enlightenment is the human being's emergence from his self-incurred minority. Minority* is inability to make use of one's own understanding without direction from another' (Kant 1996[1780]: 17).

15   Sennett cites Moynihan's statement that dependency is 'an incomplete state in life: normal in the child, abnormal in the adult' (Sennett 2003: 103). See Fraser and Gordon 1994.

16   On mechanisms, see Elster 1989 (pp. 3–10), 1998 and 1999, and Hedström and Swedberg 1998.

17   As this passage makes clear, Spinoza does not, when considering *potestas*, distinguish between domination and beneficent dependence: he assumes that all such power is dominating. This probably means that he should be included in Sennett's 'liberal canon'.

18   In making this conceptual demarcation, I agree with Foucault's (final) view that power is to be seen as relating subjects that retain some margin of freedom: he came to the view that 'without the possibility of recalcitrance, power would be equivalent to a physical determination' (Foucault 1982: 221).

19   For suggestions see the Further Reading section below.

20   According to Pasquino (Foucault's collaborator at that time), Foucault appears to have realized that his earlier treatment of power 'threatened to lead to an extremist denunciation of power – envisaged according to a repressive model' (Pasquino 1992: 79).

21 This is not exactly a new thought. As Digesser observes, 'there is a long tradition in political theory asserting a relationship between the political social context and the production of different kinds of individuals' (Digesser 1992: 991).

22 Charles Taylor comments that Foucault misses the ambivalence of the new disciplines, which 'have not served only to feed a system of control. They have also taken the form of genuine self-discipline that has made possible new kinds of collective action characterized by more egalitarian forms of participation, as recognized in the civic humanist tradition of political theory (Taylor 1984: 164).

23 As David Garland has noticed, Foucault's approach was the analytical reconstruction of historically grounded ideal types presented in an 'abstracted, perfected, fully-formed way'. He did not, as a sociologist or historian would, follow Max Weber's injunction to put them to work in empirical analysis, investigating 'the messy realm of practices and relations and the compromised, corrupted, partial ways in which these entities inhabit the real world' (Garland 1997: 199).

24 This idea, together with the pun, originated with Louis Althusser, for whom 'the subject' is both a 'centre of initiatives' and a 'subjected being'. Thus: 'the individual *is interpellated as a (free) subject in order that he shall submit (freely) to the commandments of the Subject i.e. in order that he shall freely accept his subjection*' (Althusser 1971: 169, original emphasis).

25 Similarly, Edward Said remarks that Foucault showed 'a singular lack of interest in the force of effective resistance' to power (Said 1986: 151).

26 This move was foreshadowed in an earlier interview in which Foucault, admitting that the matter was 'problematic' and his treatment of it 'intentionally uncertain', said: 'there is indeed always something in the social body, in classes, groups and individuals themselves which is some sense escapes relations of power, something which is by no means a more or less docile or reactive primal matter, but rather a centrifugal movement, an inverse energy, a discharge' (Foucault 1980b: 145, 138).

27 It seems possible that Foucault came to see this. In the late interview which we have taken to represent his 'final' views, he said: 'I think that all those notions have been ill-defined and we don't really know what we are talking about. Myself, I am not sure, when I began to interest myself in this problem of power, of having spoken very clearly about it or used the words needed. I have a much clearer idea of all that' (Foucault 1987: 19). Pasquale Pasquino informs me that Foucault became so sick of misunderstandings of his intellectual efforts that he resolved to abolish the word '*pouvoir*' from his vocabulary and replace it with '*gouvernement*' and '*gouvernementalié*'.

28 Compare what has been called Durkheim's 'socio-centric fixation' and, further, the ways in which its effect is magnified by the rhetorical force of his style of argument. As Rodney Needham once suggested to me, all the

significant propositions in his *Elementary Forms of the Religious Life* are probably false, and yet its power to generate explanations is probably unrivalled.

29 Notably the Chamber of Industry and Commerce, the Police Department and the main newspaper, which had a near monopoly of the printed press in Aalborg.

30 'The losers in the struggle over the Aalborg Project are those citizens who live, work, walk, ride their bikes, drive their cars, and use public transportation in downtown Aalborg, that is, virtually all of the city's and region's half-million inhabitants. . . . The winners are the business community in downtown Aalborg, who, via their strategy of opposing measures to restrict cars combined with grudging acceptance of improvements for public transportation, pedestrians and bicycles, have seen their customer base substantially increased' (Flvbjerg 1998: 223–4).

31 'The thought that there could be a state of communication which would be such that the games of truth could circulate freely, without obstacles, without constraint and without coercive effects, seems to me to be Utopia' (Foucault 1987: 18).

32 Judith Butler has also written of power circulating 'without voice or signature.' (Butler 1997: 6)

33 To be precise, she claims that her argument 'shares with the Foucaultian view the "hypothesis" that "Power is co-extensive with the social body; there are no spaces of primal liberty between the meshes of its network" [1980: 142]. Yet it is decidedly un-Foucaultian in its effort to elaborate critical arguments about particular relations of power and to draw distinctions grounded in democratic norms and values' (Hayward 2000: 6).

34 For the benefit of those convinced by such claims, it briefly occurred to me to change the title of this book to *Power: A Not So Radical View*.

Notes to Chapter 3   Three-Dimensional Power

1 Of course, according legitimacy to another or others is not in itself enough to render them legitimate: their actions must be consistent with established rules and roles that can be justified by prevailing norms, or beliefs shared by both dominant and subordinates who consent to the power relation (Beetham 1991: 16). On other, normative or 'objectivist', ways of defining 'legitimacy', of course, the problem does not arise.

2 Cass Sunstein, for example, has put in question the very notion of 'preferences', which is so central to economics and economics-influenced social science. The term 'preferences' is, he argues, 'highly ambiguous'.

The idea of a preference, he suggests, 'tends to disregard contextual factors that produce diverse choices in diverse settings'. It is a mistake to think of 'a preference' as 'something that lies behind choices and that is more abstract and general than choices are. What lies behind choices is not a thing but an unruly amalgam of things – aspirations, tastes, physical states, responses to existing roles and norms, values, judgments, emotions, drives, beliefs, whims – and the interactions of these forces will produce outcomes of a particular sort in accordance with the particular context. Hence we might say that *preferences are constructed, rather than elicited, by social situations*, in the sense that they are very much a function of the setting and the prevailing norms' (Sunstein 1997: 35, 38). See also Nussbaum 2000: 119–22.

3   The view is a corollary of what is sometimes called 'subjective welfarism', according to which all existing preferences are on a par for political purposes. The most minimal version of this minimalist view is probably that of F. A. Hayek, for whom whether someone is free depends on 'whether he can expect to shape his course of action in accordance with his present intentions, or whether somebody else has power so to manipulate the conditions as to make him act according to that person's will rather than his own' (Hayek 1960: 13). On such a view, the genesis and context of such present intentions has no bearing on one's freedom, which for Hayek can only be restricted by the deliberate, coercive and arbitrary intervention of another or others. Freedom, according to Hayek, is simply the 'state in which a man is not subject to coercion by the arbitrary will of another or others' (ibid., p. 11).

4   So Marx wrote that 'The advance of capitalist production develops a working class which by education, tradition and habit looks upon the requirements of that mode of production as self-evident natural laws' (Marx 1976[1867]: 899). And in *The Subjection of Women*, John Stuart Mill wrote: 'What is now called the nature of women is an eminently artificial thing – the result of forced repression in some directions, unnatural stimulation in others. It may be asserted without scruple that no other class of dependents have had their character so entirely distorted from its natural proportions by their relation with their masters. ... I consider it presumption in anyone to pretend to decide what women are or are not, can or cannot be, by natural constitution' (Mill 1989 [1869]: 38–9, 173).

5   Both Sen and Nussbaum attempt to construct (different and changing) lists of distinctively human abilities that 'exert a moral claim' (Nussbaum 2000: 83), in a way that crosses cultural boundaries and is not tied to any particular metaphysical or teleological view.

6   From *The Hindu Magazine*, 24 April 1994, quoted in Nussbaum and Glover 1995: 14. She also cites Rabindranath Tagore's 'Letter from a Wife' (1914):

In your joint family, I am known as the second daughter-in-law. All these years I have known myself as no more than that. Today, after fifteen years, as I stand alone by the sea, I know that I have another identity, which is my relationship with the universe and its creator. That gives me courage to write this letter as myself, not as the second daughter-in-law of your family.   (Epigraph in Nussbaum, 2000)

7   Fanon: 1970[1952]: 7.
8   Du Bois 1969[1903]: 45.
9   As will be evident, Scott adopts the culturalist interpretation of Gramsci's hegemony.
10 He notes that a well-known exponent of the thin version is Pierre Bourdieu, who captures it in his notion of 'naturalization'. As Bourdieu writes, 'Every established order tends to produce (to very different degrees and with very different means) the *naturalization of its own arbitrariness*' (Bourdieu 1977[1972]: 164).
11 The dominant ideology, they claim, 'has had little effect on subordinate classes. In feudalism there was a widespread cultural separation between social classes, and the peasantry had a culture quite distinct from the dominant one. In early capitalism there was little penetration of dominant conceptions into the working class. However, in late capitalism . . . there is some limited ideological incorporation of subordinate classes' alongside a 'lack of definition and unity of the ideological structure', while 'the apparatus of transmission becomes potentially more efficient with the development of the mass media and a mass compulsory education system' (Abercrombie et al. 1980: 157-8).
12 See Nussbaum 2000: Chapter 3.
13 There is, of course, an alternative interpretation of these responses to the survey: that the widows were adapting not their preferences but their behaviour, conforming to a social norm that women do not complain.
14 It is worth noticing Mill's answer to the problem of justifying the relevant counterfactual, indicating how things would be but for this exercise of power: 'if there had been a society of men in which women were not under the control of the men, something might have been positively known about the mental and moral differences which may be inherent in the nature of each' (138). See also the excellent discussion of Mill's account of infantilization and marital despotism in Urbinati 2002.
15 Bourdieu sees what he calls 'rational action theory' (of which he takes Elster as representative) as claiming alternate allegiances to a 'mechanist' and a 'teleological vision, sliding between external mechanical determinism, by causes, and intellectual determinism, by reasons – reasons of "enlightened self-interest"' (Bourdieu 2000[1997]: 139). This is unfair to Elster, who views reasons as causes and does not confine them to enlightened self-interest.

16 In support of this he cites research by Nancy Henley and Frigga Haug on the 'inculcation of the submission of the body' (p. 28).

17 Elster criticizes what he calls Bourdieu's 'semi-conspiratorial, semi-functionalist world-view (Elster 1981: 11).

18 For an excellent discussion of the issues involved, see Freund 1988.

19 See Lahire 1988: 189–219. An alternative, contrasting metaphor is to view culture as a 'tool-kit' (Swidler 1986).

20 See Chapter 2 above.

21 I owe this example to Clarissa Hayward.

22 She quotes an illiterate 'elderly toothless woman' who had 'recently gone with a group to Delhi', saying that such women were 'not really like women, but more like "sheep and buffaloes"' (Nussbaum 2000: 43).

23 But, Mill wrote,

> it will be said, the rule of men differs from all these others in not being a rule of force; it is accepted voluntarily; women make no complaint, and are consenting parties to it. In the first place, a great number of women do not accept it. Ever since there have been women able to make their sentiments known by their writings (the only mode of publicity which society permits to them), an increasing number of them have recorded protests against their present social condition.   (Mill 1989[1869]: 131)

He might, for instance, have cited Wollstonecraft 1988[1792].

24 To quote Mill again:

> It is a political law of nature that those who are under any power of ancient origin, never begin by complaining of the power itself, but only of its oppressive exercise. There is never any want of women who complain of ill usage by their husbands. There would be infinitely more, if complaint were not the greatest of all provocations to a repetition and increase of the ill usage. It is this which frustrates all attempts to maintain the power but protect the woman against its abuses.   (1989[1869]: 132)

GUIDE TO
FURTHER READING

Conceptual Analyses

The best, most acute and systematic analytical discussion of the concept of power is Morriss 2002 – although it focuses entirely on 'power to', devoting only a few sentences in the Introduction to the second edition to 'power over', the author having been persuaded of the importance of domination by Pettit 1997 but, curiously, admitting to a 'distaste' for the topic (p. xxxiv). Morriss is criticized in Barry 1988 and Dowding 1990, 1991 and 1996, but effectively answers these criticisms in the new introduction. Other valuable conceptual discussions of the concept of power are Riker 1964, March 1966, White 1971 and 1972, Goldman 1972, 1974a and 1974b (but see Braybrooke 1973), Ball 1975, 1979 and 1988a, Elster 1976 (pp. 249–54), Oppenheim 1981, Airaksinen 1984, 1988 and 1992, Stoppino 1995, and Ledyaev 1997. On coercion, see Nozick 1972, Pennock and Chapman (eds) 1972, and Wertheimer 1987; on authority, see Raz 1979 and Raz (ed.) 1990; on autonomy, see Haworth 1986, Hill 1987, Dworkin 1988 and Friedman 2003; on manipulation see Riker 1986; and on the concept of interests, see Balbus 1971, Connolly 1972 and, especially, Feinberg 1984. Despite its title, Nagel 1975 is a study of influence, not power: it explores ways of defining, measuring and inferring the causal influence of preferences upon outcomes. Recent writings on 'mechanisms' include Boudon 1998, Elster 1998 and 1999, Hedström and Swedberg (eds) 1998, and van den Berg 1998.

General Works

General works that cover the topic and the debates around it are Dennis Wrong's magisterial survey (Wrong 1979), Clegg 1975, Martin 1977 and 1989, Dyrberg 1997, Haugaard 1997 and Scott 2001. There are various 'readers' – collections of reprinted articles and chapters from books on the topic: Bell, Edwards and Harrison Wagner (ed.) 1969, Lukes (ed.) 1986, Haugaard (ed.) 2002 and, most extensively in three volumes, Scott (ed.) 1994. There are also collections of newly published articles by various hands that relate the concept of power to currently debated issues, theoretical and empirical, at the time of publication, notably Cartwright (ed.) 1959, Champlin (ed.) 1971, Barry (ed.) 1976, Wartenberg (ed.) 1992 and Goverde, Cerny, Haugaard and Lentner (eds) 2000.

Essential Contestedness

On the question of whether power is an 'essentially contested concept', endorsed in Lukes 1974 and Connolly 1983, there are various contributions. The originating proponent of essential contestedness was W. B. Gallie in Gallie 1955–6. Among the sceptical, see Barry 1975, MacDonald 1976 (but see Lukes 1977a) and Morriss 1980, and among the advocates Gray 1977 and 1983. For carefully reasoned defences of the essential contestedness of political concepts, see Swanton 1985 and Mason 1993.

Classical Statements

Among classical treatments of power alluded to in the text, the reader can consult Boétie 1998[1548], Hobbes 1946[1651], Spinoza 1958[1670 and 1677], Locke 1946[1690] and 1975[1690], Vico 1963[1744], Kant 1996[1780], Burke 1910[1790], Wollstonecraft 1988[1792], Marx 1976[1867], Marx and Engels 1962 and 1965[1845], Mill 1989[1869], and Nietzsche 1956 [1887], 1967[1908], 1968[1906] and 1974[1882, 1887].

Modern Statements

Twentieth-century conceptions of power have been massively influenced by Max Weber's classic definitions and deployment of the concepts of power (*Macht*) and domination (*Herrschaft*) and by his accounts of the modes of legitimate domination (Weber 1978[1910–14]), on which last topic see Beetham 1991. Weber did not influence Bertrand Russell whose book on power (Russell 1938) lucidly discusses forms and types of power, ranges across history and is full of insights, but is, however, quite innocent of social science. Hannah Arendt focused on power in her short study of violence, defining power in distinction to the Weberian language of domination in Arendt 1970 and was criticized in *PRV* and in Habermas 1977. Pioneering social scientific treatments were Lasswell and Kaplan 1950 for political scientists, and for sociologists Parsons 1963a, 1963b and 1967 (soundly criticized for eschewing both domination and conflict in Giddens 1968), and for students of stratification Lenski 1966, and of exchange theory Blau 1986. Barry Barnes, one of the founders of the Edinburgh school of the sociology of science, published a study of power that explores its relation to knowledge in Barnes 1988 (see also Barnes 1993). In the German-speaking world there are Popitz 1986 and Niklas Luhmann's application of his distinctive version of systems theory to the topic in Luhmann 1975 and, from the standpoint of Critical Theory, Honneth 1991. Political sociological studies of power include Michael Mann's magisterial work in comparative historical sociology in Mann 1986 and 1993 and Poggi's Weberian study of political, ideological and economic power in relation to the state in Poggi 2001. The 'power resources' approach is set out in Korpi 1985, an 'economic' approach in Barry 1974 and 1989, one version of the rational choice approach in Dowding 1991 and 1996, and another more sociological version in Coleman 1974, 1982 and 1990 (but see Lukes 2003), a game theory approach in Balzer 1992 and a political linguistics approach in Bell 1975. Anthropological treatments of power include Tambiah 1968, Cohen 1974, Farndon (ed.) 1985, Bell 1992, and

Wolf 1999 and 2001. Kertzer 1988 is an interesting study of ritual and power. Professional economists, interestingly enough, have had little that is interesting to say about power, as can be seen by consulting Rothschild (ed.) 1971, and reflecting on the absence of other such collections, although two notable twentieth-century economists have written thoughtful books on the topic, namely Galbraith 1983 and Boulding 1989. For an extended discussion by a philosopher of the ideas of voluntary servitude and false consciousness, see Rosen 1996. For treatments of power by international relations specialists, see White 1978, Baldwin 1989, Strange 1990 and (in ways that connect with this book's themes) Guzzini 1993.

Major Debates

Talcott Parsons (Parsons 1957) crossed swords with C. Wright Mills (Mills 1956) about whether there was a 'power elite' dominating American democracy. A subsequent debate, also centring on issues of structure versus agency, began in the late 1960s between two Marxists, Ralph Miliband in Britain and Nicos Poulantzas in France. Miliband's key book was Miliband 1969 and Poulantzas's was Poulantzas 1973 (published in French in 1968); their debate, in the *New Left Review*, is to found in Poulantzas 1969 and 1976, and Miliband 1970 and 1973. The debate was joined in 1975 by Laclau (Laclau 1975) and discussed in Gold, Lo and Wright 1975 and Clarke 1977. The work of Michel Foucault, aside from its untraceably manifold progeny of epigones, interpreters and critics (see below), also inspired a brief but interesting debate with Jürgen Habermas, the main contributions to which are reproduced and discussed in Kelly (ed.) 1994 and Ashenden and Owen (eds) 1999.

As explained in the Introduction, the 'faces of power' debate grew out of the critique of the 'elite' theories of Mills 1956 and Hunter 1953. Inaugurated by Dahl 1957 and 1958, its first phase issued in Dahl 1961 (for his later statements see Dahl 1968 and 1976), Polsby 1963 (and see Polsby 1968). Criticized in Bachrach and Baratz 1962, 1963 (reprinted in their empirical study Bachrach and Baratz 1970), the debate was joined by Merelman 1968a and 1968b, Wolfinger 1971a and 1971b, Frey 1971, and Debnam 1975 and 1984, and responded to in Bachrach and Baratz 1968 and 1975. *PRV* joined the fray in 1974, citing in support Crenson's study of air pollution in two US cities (Crenson 1971) and was in turn given empirical application in various studies, among them Gaventa 1980, Danziger 1988 and Komter 1989. The subsequent debate over a range of relevant issues continues until now, and many of the contributions contain trenchant critiques of *PRV*, among them Barry 1975, Clegg 1975, Ball 1976, Bilgrami 1976, Bradshaw 1976, Hindess 1976, Abell 1977, Goldman 1977, Thomas 1978, Young 1978, Bloch et al. 1979, Benton 1981, Hoy 1981, Hindess 1982, Hartsock 1983, Layder 1985, Barbalet 1987, Isaac 1987a and 1987b, Morriss 2002 (first edition 1987), West 1987, Ball 1988b, Clegg 1989, Kernohan 1989, Digesser 1992, Hyland 1995, Haugaard 1997, Hay, 1997, Doyle 1998, Hay 1999 and 2002, Hayward 2000, which combines theory and an excellent empirical case study discussed in Chapter 2, and McGettigan 2002. A very useful selection from these contributions is to be found in Scott (ed.) 1994, and useful summaries in several places, including Scott 2001 and Haugaard (ed.) 2002.

Gramsci and Hegemony

As indicated in the Introduction, *PRV* made the connection between this debate and the Gramscian notion of hegemony. From the large literature on that topic, the following are relevant to its treatment here: Anderson 1976–7, Gramsci 1971[1926–37], Przeworski 1980 and 1998, Abercrombie, Hill and Turner 1980, Femia 1981, Bates, 1975 and Williams 1960. In Scott 1985 and 1990, James Scott contends that the concept is unhelpful for the study of domination; for critiques of Scott, see Mitchell 1990, Tilly 1991 and Farber 2000.

Feminism and Power

There are many books and articles that discuss power in the light of feminist ideas, notably Allen 1999, Bordo 2003, Butler 1997, Connell 1987, Fraser 1989, Hartsock 1983 and 1984, Held 1993, Janeway 1981, Miller 1992, Nussbaum 2000, Okin 1989 and I. M. Young 1988 and 1990. There are also those with a particular focus on the bearing of Foucault's ideas on feminism and feminist issues, which include Bartky 1990, Diamond and Quinby (eds) 1988, Fraser 1981, Hekman (ed.) 1996, McNay 1992, Sawicki 1991 and Spivak 1992.

Foucault

Foucault's shorter writings and his interviews on the topic are collected in Foucault 2000, and other central texts are Foucault 1978[1975], 1980a, 1980b, 1980c[1976], 1982 and 1987. Concerning Foucault's treatment of power, the following are interesting discussions and/or developments: Connolly 1991, Donzelot 1979, Flyvbjerg 1994, Fraser and Gordon 1994, Garland 1990 and 1997, Hacking 1986, Hindess 1996, Hoy (ed.) 1986, McHoul and Grace 1993, Merquior 1991, Pasquino 1992, Rose 1999 and Taylor 1984.

Bourdieu

Among Bourdieu's many writings, those most focused on power and domination are Bourdieu 1977[1972], 1984[1979], 1989 [1987], 1990[1980], 1991, 2000[1997] and 2001[1998]. Elster 1981 and Lahire 1998 offer interesting critical perspectives on Bourdieu's explanatory approach.

REFERENCES

Abell, P. (1977) 'The Many Faces of Power and Liberty: Revealed Preferences, Autonomy and Teleological Explanation', *Sociology*, 11: 3–24.

Abercrombie, N., Hill, S. and Turner, B. (1980) *The Dominant Ideology Thesis*. London: Allen & Unwin.

Airaksinen, T. (1984) 'Coercion, Deterrence and Authority', *Theory and Decision*, 17: 105–17.

Airaksinen, T. (1988) *The Ethics of Coercion and Authority*. Pittsburgh, PA: Pittsburgh University Press.

Airaksinen, T. (1992) 'The Rhetoric of Domination', in Wartenberg (ed.) 1992: 102–20.

Allen, A. (1999) *The Power of Feminist Theory: Domination, Resistance, Solidarity*. Boulder, CO: Westview Press.

Althusser, L. (1971) 'Ideology and Ideological State Apparatuses', in *Lenin and Philosophy and Other Essays*, trans. Ben Brewster. London: New Left Books.

Althusser, L. and Balibar, E. (1968) *Lire le Capital*. Paris: Maspero.

Anderson, P. (1976–7) 'The Antinomies of Antonio Gramsci', *New Left Review*, 100: 5–78.

Arendt, H. (1970) *On Violence*. London: Allen Lane.

Aron, R. (1964) '*Macht*, power, *puissance*: prose démocratique ou poésie démonaique?', *Archives européennes de sociologie* (*European Journal of Sociology*), 5: 25–51; reprinted in Lukes (ed.) 1986.

Ashenden, S. and Owen, D. (eds) (1999) *Foucault contra Habermas: Recasting the Dialogue between Genealogy and Critical Theory*. London: Sage.

Bachrach, P. (1967) *The Theory of Democratic Elitism: A Critique*. Boston, MA: Little, Brown.

Bachrach, P. and Baratz, M. S. (1962) 'The Two Faces of Power', *American Political Science Review*, 56: 941–52; reprinted in Bachrach and Baratz 1970, Bell et al. 1969, and Scott (ed.) 1994.

References

Bachrach, P. and Baratz, M. S. (1963) 'Decisions and Nondecisions: An Analytical Framework', *American Political Science Review*, 57: 641–51; reprinted in Bachrach and Baratz 1970, Bell et al. 1969, and Scott (ed.) 1994.

Bachrach, P. and Baratz, M. S. (1968) Communication to the Editor, *American Political Science Review*, 62: 1268–9.

Bachrach, P. and Baratz, M. S. (1970) *Power and Poverty: Theory and Practice*. New York: Oxford University Press.

Bachrach, P. and Baratz, M. S. (1975) 'Power and its Two Faces Revisited: A Reply to Geoffrey Debnam', *American Political Science Review*, 69: 900–4; reprinted in Scott (ed.) 1994.

Bachrach, P. and Bergman, E. (1973) *Power and Choice: The Formulation of American Foreign Policy*. Lexington, MA: Lexington Books, D. C. Heath.

Bachrach, P. and Botwinick, A. (1992) *Power and Empowerment: A Radical Theory of Participatory Democracy*. Philadelphia, PA: Temple University Press.

Balbus, I. D. (1971) 'The Concept of Interest in Pluralist and Marxist Analysis', *Politics and Society*, 1: 151–77.

Baldwin, D. A. (1989) *Paradoxes of Power*. Oxford: Basil Blackwell.

Ball, T. (1975) 'Models of Power: Past and Present', *Journal of the History of the Behavioral Sciences*, 11: 211–22.

Ball, T. (1976) Review of S. Lukes, *Power: A Radical View* and Nagel 1975, *Political Theory*, 4: 246–9.

Ball, T. (1979) 'Power, Causation and Explanation', *Polity*, 8: 189–214.

Ball, T. (1988a) *Transforming Political Discourse*. Oxford: Basil Blackwell.

Ball, T. (1988b) 'New Faces of Power' (Chapter 4 of Ball 1988); reprinted in slightly revised form in Wartenberg (ed.) 1992.

Balzer, W. (1992) 'Game Theory and Power Theory: A Critical Comparison', in Wartenberg (ed.) 1992: 56–78.

Barbalet, J. M. (1987) 'Power, Structural Resources and Agency', *Perspectives in Social Theory*, 8: 1–24.

Barnes, B. (1988) *The Nature of Power*. Cambridge: Polity Press.

Barnes, B. (1993) 'Power', in R. Bellamy, (ed.), *Theories and Concepts of Politics: An Introduction*. Manchester: Manchester University Press.

Barry, B. (1965) *Political Argument*. London: Routledge & Kegan Paul.

References

Barry, B. (1974) 'The Economic Approach to the Analysis of Power and Conflict', *Government and Opposition*, 9: 189–223.

Barry, B. (1975) 'The Obscurities of Power', *Government and Opposition*, 10: 250–4; reprinted in Barry 1989.

Barry, B. (ed.) (1976) *Power and Political Theory: Some European Perspectives*. London and New York: John Wiley.

Barry, B. (1988) 'The Uses of "Power"', *Government and Opposition*, 23: 340–53; reprinted in Barry 1989.

Barry, B. (1989) *Democracy, Power and Justice*. Oxford: Clarendon Press.

Bartky, S. (1990) 'Foucault, Femininity and the Modernization of Patriarchal Power', in S. Bartky, *Femininity and Domination*. New York: Routledge.

Bates, T. R. (1975) 'Gramsci and the Theory of Hegemony', *Journal of the History of Ideas*, 36(2): 351–66.

Beetham, D. (1991) *The Legitimation of Power*. Basingstoke: Macmillan.

Bell, C. (1992) *Ritual Theory, Ritual Practice*, Part III: 'Ritual and Power'. New York and Oxford: Oxford University Press.

Bell, D. V. J. (1975) *Power, Influence and Authority: An Essay in Political Linguistics*. New York: Oxford University Press.

Bell, R., Edwards, D. V. and Harrison Wagner, R. (1969) *Political Power: A Reader in Theory and Research*. New York: Free Press.

Benn, S. (1967) 'Freedom and Persuasion', *Australasian Journal of Philosophy*, 45: 259–75.

Benton, T. (1981) ' "Objective" Interests and the Sociology of Power', *Sociology*, 15: 161–84; reprinted in Scott (ed.) 1994.

Bilgrami, A. (1976) 'Lukes on Power and Behaviouralism', *Inquiry*, 10, 2: 267–74.

Blau, P. (1986) *Exchange and Power in Social Life*, 2nd edn. New Brunswick, NJ: Transaction Books.

Bloch, M. et al. (1979) 'Power in Social Theory: A Non-Relative View', in S. C. Brown (ed.), *Philosophical Disputes in the Social Sciences*, pp. 243–59. Sussex: Harvester.

Boétie, E. de La (1998[1548]) 'On Voluntary Servitude', trans. D. L. Schaefer, in D. L Schaefer (ed.), *Freedom over Servitude: Montaigne, La Boétie, and 'On Voluntary Servitude'*, first published (in Latin) 1574. Westport, CT: Greenwood Press.

Bordo, S. (2003) *Unbearable Weight: Feminism, Western Culture and the Body*, 10th Anniversary Edition with new preface by the author, new foreword by Leslie Heywood. Berkeley, CA: University of California Press; 1st edn 1993.

References

Boudon, R. (1998) 'Social Mechanisms without Black Boxes', in Hedström and Swedberg (eds) 1998.

Boulding, K. E. (1989) *Three Faces of Power*. Newbury Park, CA, and London: Sage.

Bourdieu, P. (1977[1972]) *Outlines of a Theory of Practice*, trans. Richard Nice. Cambridge: Cambridge University Press.

Bourdieu, P. (1984[1979]) *Distinction: A Social Critique of the Judgment of Taste*, trans. Richard Nice. Cambridge, MA: Harvard University Press.

Bourdieu, P. (1989[1987]) 'Social Space and Symbolic Power', *Sociological Theory*, 7: 14–25; originally published in *Choses dites*, Paris: Editions de Minuit, 1987.

Bourdieu, P. (1990[1980]) *The Logic of Practice*, trans. Richard Nice. Stanford, CA: Stanford University Press.

Bourdieu, P. (1991) *Language and Symbolic Power: The Economy of Linguistic Exchanges*, ed. and introduced by J. B. Thompson. Cambridge: Polity Press.

Bourdieu, P. (2000[1997]) *Pascalian Meditations*, trans. Richard Nice. Stanford, CA: Stanford University Press.

Bourdieu, P. (2001[1998]) *Masculine Domination*, trans. Richard Nice. Stanford, CA: Stanford University Press.

Bowles, S. and Gintis, H. (1992) 'The Political Economy of Contested Exchange' in Wartenberg (ed.) 1992: 196–224.

Bradshaw, A. (1976) 'A Critique of Steven Lukes' *Power: A Radical View*', *Sociology*, 10: 121–7; reprinted in Scott (ed.) 1994.

Braybrooke, D. (1973) 'Two Blown Fuses in Goldman's Analysis of Power', *Philosophical Studies*, 24(6): 369–77.

Brubaker, R. and Cooper, F. (2000) 'Beyond Identity', *Theory and Society*, 29: 1–47.

Burke, E. (1910 [1790]) *Reflections on the Revolution in France*. London: Dent, Everyman Library.

Butler, J. (1997) *The Psychic Life of Power: Theories in Subjection*. Stanford, CA: Stanford University Press.

Cartwright, D. (ed.) (1959) *Studies in Social Power*. Ann Arbor, MI: University of Michigan Press.

Champlin, J. R (ed.) (1971) *Power*. New York: W. W. Norton.

Clarke, S. (1977) 'Marxism, Sociology and Poulantzas's Theory of the State', *Capital and Class*, 2: 1–31.

Clegg, S. R. (1975) *Power, Rule and Domination*. London: Routledge.

Clegg, S. R. (1989) *Frameworks of Power*. London: Sage.

References

Cohen, A. (1974) *Two-Dimensional Man: An Essay on the Anthropology of Power and Symbolism in Complex Society*. London: Routledge & Kegan Paul.

Coleman, J. S. (1974) *Power and the Structure of Society*. New York and London: W. W. Norton.

Coleman, J. S. (1982) *The Asymmetric Society*. Syracuse, NY: Syracuse University Press.

Coleman, J. S. (1990) *The Foundations of Social Theory*. Cambridge, MA: Harvard University Press.

Connell, R. W. (1987) *Gender and Power: Society, the Person and Sexual Politics*. Stanford, CA: Standford University Press.

Connolly, W. E. (1972) 'On "Interests" in Politics', *Politics and Society*, 2: 459–77; reprinted in Connolly 1983.

Connolly, W. E. (1983) *The Terms of Political Discourse*, 2nd edn. Oxford: Martin Robertson; 1st edn 1974.

Connolly, W. E. (1991) *Identity/Difference*. Ithaca, NY: Cornell University Press.

Crenson, M. A. (1971) *The Un-Politics of Air Pollution: A Study of Non-Decisionmaking in the Cities*. Baltimore, MD: Johns Hopkins Press.

Dahl, R. A. (1957) 'The Concept of Power', *Behavioral Science*, 2: 201–15; reprinted in Scott (ed.) 1994.

Dahl, R. A. (1958) 'A Critique of the Ruling Elite Model', *American Political Science Review*, 52: 463–9.

Dahl, R. A. (1961) *Who Governs? Democracy and Power in an American City*. New Haven, CT: Yale University Press.

Dahl, R. A. (1968) 'Power', *International Encyclopedia of the Social Sciences*, ed. D. L. Sills. New York: Crowell, Collier and Macmillan; reprinted in Lukes (ed.) 1986.

Dahl, R. A. (1976) *Modern Political Analysis*, 3rd edn. Englewood Cliffs, NJ: Prentice-Hall.

Dahrendorf, R. (1959) *Class and Class Conflict in Industrial Society*. London: Routledge & Kegan Paul.

Danziger, R. (1988) *Political Powerlessness: Agricultural Workers in Post-war England*. Manchester: Manchester University Press.

Debnam, G. (1975) 'Nondecisions and Power: The Two Faces of Bachrach and Baratz', *American Political Science Review*, 69: 889–900.

Debnam, G. (1984) *The Analysis of Power: A Realist Approach*. Basingstoke: Macmillan.

Diamond, I. and Quinby, L. (eds) (1988) *Feminism and Foucault: Reflections on Resistance*. Boston, MA: Northeastern University Press.

References

Digesser, P. (1992) 'The Fourth Face of Power', *Journal of Politics*, 54, 4: 977–1007.

Domhoff, G. W. (1978) *Who Really Rules? New Haven and Community Power Reexamined.* New Brunswick, NJ: Transaction Books.

Donzelot, J. (1979) *The Policing of Families.* New York: Pantheon.

Dowding, K. M. (1990) 'Ability and Aldeness: Morriss on Power and Counteractuals', *Government Department Working Papers*, 10. Uxbridge: Brunel University.

Dowding, K. M. (1991) *Rational Choice and Political Power.* London: Edward Elgar.

Dowding, K. M. (1996) *Power.* Minneapolis, MN: University of Minnesota Press.

Doyle, J. (1998) 'Power and Contentment', *Politics*, 18(1): 49–56.

Du Bois, W. E. B. (1969[1903]) *The Souls of Black Folk.* New York: New American Library.

Duncan, G. and Lukes, S. (1964) 'The New Democracy', *Political Studies*, 11(2): 156–77.

Dworkin, G. (1988) *The Theory and Practice of Autonomy.* Cambridge: Cambridge University Press.

Dyrberg, T. B. (1997) *The Circular Structure of Power: Politics, Identity, Community.* London: Verso.

Elster, J. (1976) 'Some Conceptual Problems in Political Theory', in Barry (ed.) 1976, pp. 243–70.

Elster, J. (1981) 'Snobs' (review of Bourdieu 1984[1979]). *London Review of Books*, 3(20): 10–12.

Elster, J. (1983) *Sour Grapes: Studies in the Subversion of Rationality.* Cambridge: Cambridge University Press.

Elster, J. (1989) *Nuts and Bolts for the Social Sciences.* Cambridge: Cambridge University Press.

Elster, J. (1998) 'A Plea for Mechanisms', in P. Hedström and R. Swedberg (eds), *Social Mechanisms: An Analytical Approach to Social Theory.* Cambridge: Cambridge University Press, pp. 45–73.

Elster, J. (1999) *Alchemies of the Mind: Rationality and the Emotions.* Cambridge and New York: Cambridge University Press.

Fanon, F. (1970[1952]) *Black Skin, White Masks*, trans. C. L. Markmann. London: Paladin.

Farber, S. (2000) *Social Decay and Transformation: A View from the Left.* Lanham, MD: Lexington Books.

Farndon, R. (ed.) (1985) *Power and Knowledge: Anthropological and Sociological Approaches.* Edinburgh: Scottish Academic Press.

References

Feinberg, J. (1984) *Harm to Others: The Moral Limits of the Criminal Law*. New York and Oxford: Oxford University Press.

Femia, J. (1981) *Gramsci's Political Thought: Hegemony, Consciousness and the Revolutionary Process*. Oxford: Clarendon Press.

Flyvbjerg, B. (1998) *Rationality and Power: Democracy in Practice*. Chicago, IL: Chicago University Press.

Foucault, M. (1978[1975]) *Discipline and Punish: The Birth of the Prison*, trans. Alan Sheridan. New York: Random House.

Foucault, M. (1980a) *Power/Knowledge: Selected Interviews and Other Writings, 1972–77*. Brighton: Harvester.

Foucault M. (1980b) 'Power and Strategies', in Foucault 1980a. New York: Pantheon.

Foucault, M. (1980c[1976]) *The History of Sexuality*, vol. 1, trans. Robert Hurley. New York: Random House.

Foucault, M. (1982) 'The Subject and Power' published as the Afterword to H. L. Dreyfus and P. Rabinow, *Michel Foucault: Beyond Structuralism and Hermeneutics*. Brighton: Harvester; Chicago, IL: Chicago University Press, pp. 208–26; reprinted in Foucault 2000.

Foucault, M. (1987) 'The Ethic of Care for the Self as a Practice of Freedom: an Interview with Michel Foucault on 20 January 1984', in J. Bernauer and D. Rasmussen (eds), *The Final Foucault*. Cambridge, MA and London: MIT Press.

Foucault, M. (2000) *Power*, ed. J. D. Faubion as vol. 3 of *Essential Works of Foucault, 1954–1884*. New York: New Press.

Fraser, N. (1981) 'Foucault on Modern Power: Empirical Insights and Normative Confusions', *Praxis International*, 1: 272–87; reprinted in Fraser 1989.

Fraser, N. (1989) *Unruly Practices: Power, Gender and Discourse in Contemporary Critical Theory*. Cambridge: Polity Press.

Fraser, N. (1997) *Justice Interruptus: Critical Reflections on the 'Postsocialist' Condition*. New York and London: Routledge.

Fraser, N. and Gordon, L. (1994) ' "A Genealogy of "Dependency": Tracing a Keyword of the US Welfare State', *Signs*, 19: 311–36; reprinted in Fraser 1997.

Freund, P. E. S. (1988) 'Bringing Society into the Body: Understanding Socialized Human Nature', *Theory and Society*, 17(6): 838–64.

Frey, F. W. (1971) 'Comment: On Issues and Nonissues in the Study of Power', *American Political Science Review* 65: 1081–1101.

Friedman, M. (2003) *Autonomy, Gender, Politics*. Oxford: Oxford University Press.

References

Friedrich, C. J. (1941) *Constitutional Government and Democracy: Theory and Practice in Europe and America*. Boston, MA: Ginn.

Galbraith, J. K. (1983) *The Anatomy of Power*. Boston, MA: Houghton Mifflin.

Gallie, W. B. (1955–6) 'Essentially Contested Concepts', *Proceedings of the Aristotelian Society*, 56: 167–98.

Garland, D. (1990) *Punishment and Modern Society: A Study in Social Theory*. Oxford: Clarendon Press.

Garland, D. (1997) ' "Governmentality" and the Problem of Crime', *Theoretical Criminology*, 1: 173–214.

Gaventa, J. (1980) *Power and Powerlessness: Quiescence and Rebellion in an Appalachian Valley*. Oxford: Clarendon Press.

Geras, N. (1983) *Marx and Human Nature*. London: New Left Books.

Giddens, A. (1968) ' "Power" in the Recent Writings of Talcott Parsons', *Sociology*, 2: 257–72.

Gold, D., Lo, C. and Wright, E. O. (1975) 'Recent Developments in Marxist Theories of the Capitalist State', *Monthly Review*, 27: 29–43, 46–51.

Goldman, A. (1972) 'Towards a Theory of Social Power', *Philosophical Studies*, 23: 221–68; reprinted in Lukes (ed.) 1986.

Goldman, A. (1974a) 'On the Measurement of Power', *Journal of Philosophy*, 71: 231–52.

Goldman, A. (1974b) 'Power, Time and Cost', *Philosophical Studies*, 26: 263–70.

Goldman, A. (1977) 'Steven Lukes, *Power: A Radical View*', *Theory and Decision*, 8: 305–10.

Goverde, H., Cerny, P. G., Haugaard, M. and Lentner, H. M. (eds) (2000) *Power in Contemporary Politics: Theories, Practices, Globalizations*. London: Sage.

Gramsci, A. (1971[1926–37]) *Selections from the Prison Notebooks of Antonio Gramsci*, ed. Q. Hoare and G. Nowell-Smith. London: Lawrence & Wishart.

Gray, J. (1977) 'On the Contestability of Social and Political Concepts', *Political Theory*, 5: 331–48.

Gray, J. (1983) 'Political Power, Social Theory and Essential Contestability', in D. Miller and L. Siedentop (eds), *The Nature of Political Theory*, Oxford: Clarendon Press, pp. 75–101.

Guzzini, S. (1993) 'Structural Power: the Limits of Neorealist Power Analysis', *International Organization*, 47: 443–78.

References

Habermas, J. (1977) 'Hannah Arendt's Communications Concept of Power', *Social Research*, 44, 3–24; reprinted in Lukes (ed.) 1986.

Hacking, I. (1986) 'Making up People', in T. Heller, M. Sosna and D. Wellbery (eds), *Reconstructing Individualism*. Stanford, CA: Stanford University Press.

Harré, R. and Madden, E. H. (1975) *Causal Powers*. Oxford: Basil Blackwell.

Hartsock, N. C. M. (1983) *Money, Sex and Power: Toward a Feminist Historical Materialism*. New York and London: Longman.

Hartsock, N. C. M. (1984) 'Gender and Sexuality: Masculinity, Violence and Domination', *Humanities in Society*, 7: 19–45; reprinted in Wartenberg (ed.) 1992.

Haugaard, M. (1997) *The Constitution of Power: A Theoretical Analysis of Power, Knowledge and Structure*. Manchester: Manchester University Press.

Haugaard, M. (ed.) (2002) *Power: A Reader*. Manchester: Manchester University Press.

Haworth, L. (1986) *Autonomy: An Essay in Philosophical Psychology and Ethics*. New Haven, CT: Yale University Press.

Hay, C. (1997) 'Divided by a Common Language: Political Theory and the Concept of Power', *Politics*, 17(1): 45–52.

Hay, C. (1999) 'Still Divided by a Common Language: Discontentment and the Semantics of Power', *Politics*, 19(1): 47–50.

Hay, C. (2002) *Political Analysis: A Critical Introduction*. Basingstoke: Palgrave Macmillan.

Hayek, F. A. (1960) *The Constitution of Liberty*. London: Routledge & Kegan Paul.

Hayward, C. R. (2000) *De-facing Power*. Cambridge: Cambridge University Press.

Hedström, P. and Swedberg, R. (eds) (1998) *Social Mechanisms: An Analytical Approach to Social Theory*. Cambridge: Cambridge University Press.

Hekman, S. (ed.) (1996) *Re-reading the Canon: Feminist Interpretations of Foucault*. University Park, PA: Pennsylvania State Press.

Held, V. (1993) *Feminist Morality: Transforming Culture, Society and Politics*. Chicago, IL: Chicago University Press.

Hill, T. E. (1987) *Autonomy and Self-Respect*. Cambridge: Cambridge University Press.

References

Hindess, B. (1976) 'On Three-Dimensional Power', *Political Studies*, 24: 329–33.

Hindess, B. (1982) 'Power, Interests and the Outcomes of Struggles', *Sociology*, 16: 498–511; reprinted in Scott (ed.) 1994.

Hindess, B. (1996) *Discourses of Power: From Hobbes to Foucault*. Oxford: Blackwell Publishing.

Hobbes, T. (1946[1651]) *Leviathan*, ed. with an introduction by M. Oakeshott. Oxford: Basil Blackwell.

Honneth, A. (1991) *The Critique of Power: Reflective Stages in a Critical Social Theory*, trans. K. Baynes. Cambridge, MA: MIT Press.

Hoy, D. C. (1981) 'Power, Repression, Progress: Foucault, Lukes and the Frankfurt School', *TriQuarterly*, 52(Fall) 43–63; reprinted in Hoy (ed.) 1986.

Hoy, D. C. (ed.) (1986) *Foucault: A Critical Reader*. Oxford: Basil Blackwell.

Hunter, F. (1953) *Community Power Structure: A Study of Decision Makers*. Chapel Hill, NC: University of North Caroline Press.

Hyland, J. L. (1995) *Democratic Theory: The Philosophical Foundations*. Manchester: Manchester University Press.

Isaac, J. C. (1987a) 'Beyond the Three Faces of Power', *Polity*, 20: 4–30; reprinted in Wartenberg (ed.) 1992.

Isaac, J. C. (1987b) *Power and Marxist Theory: A Realist View*. Ithaca, NY: Cornell University Press.

Isaacs, H. R. (1964) *India's Ex-Untouchables*. New York: John Day.

Janeway, E. (1981) *The Powers of the Weak*. New York: Morrow Quill Paperbacks.

Kant, I. (1996[1780]) 'Answer to the Question "What is Enlightenment?"', in I. Kant, *Practical Philosophy*, trans. and ed. M. J. Gregor. Cambridge: Cambridge University Press.

Kelly, M. (ed.) (1994) *Critique and Power: Recasting the Foucault/Habermas Debate*. Cambridge, MA: MIT Press.

Kenny, A. (1975) *Will, Freedom and Power*. Oxford: Basil Blackwell.

Kernohan, A. (1989) 'Social Power and Human Agency', *Journal of Philosophy*, 86 (12): 712–26.

Kertzer, D. I. (1988) *Ritual, Politics and Power*. New Haven, CT: Yale University Press.

Knights, D. and Wilmott, H. (1982) 'Power, Values and Relations: a Comment on Benton', *Sociology*, 16: 578–85.

Komter, A. (1989) 'Hidden Power in Marriage', *Gender and Society*, 3(2): 187–219.

References

Korpi, W. (1985) 'Power Resources Approach vs. Action and Conflict: On Causal and Intentional Explanations in the Study of Power', *Sociological Theory*, 3: 31–45.

Laclau, E. (1975) 'The Specificity of the Political: Around the Poulantzas–Miliband Debate', *Economy and Society*, 5(1): 87–110.

Lahire, B. (1998) *L'Homme pluriel: les ressorts de l'action*. Paris: Nathan.

Lasswell, H. and Kaplan, A. (1950) *Power and Society*. New Haven, CT: Yale University Press.

Latour, B. (1986) 'The Powers of Association' in Law (ed.) 1986: 264–80.

Law, J. A. (ed.) (1986) *Power, Action and Belief: A New Sociology of Knowledge?* Sociological Review Monographs, 32: London: Routledge & Kegan Paul.

Layder, D. (1985) 'Power, Structure and Agency', *Journal for the Theory of Social Behaviour*, 15: 131–49; reprinted in Scott (ed.) 1994.

Ledyaev, V. G. (1997) *Power: A Conceptual Analysis*. Commack, NY: Nova Science.

Leiter, B. (2002) *Nietzsche on Morality*. London: Routledge.

Lenski, G. E. (1966) *Power and Privilege: A Theory of Social Stratification*. New York: McGraw Hill.

Lewis, B. (ed.) (1967) *The Encyclopedia of Islam*, new edn. Leiden: Brill; London: Luzac.

Lipsitz, L. (1970) 'On Political Belief: the Grievances of the Poor', in P. Green and S. Levinson (eds), *Power and Community: Dissenting Essays in Political Science*. New York: Random House, Vintage Books.

Locke, J. (1946[1690]) *The Second Treatise on Civil Government* and *A Letter Concerning Toleration*, ed. J. W. Gough. Oxford: Basil Blackwell.

Locke, J. (1975[1690]) *An Essay Concerning Human Understanding*, ed. P. H. Nidditch. Oxford: Clarendon Press.

Luhmann, N. (1975) *Macht*. Stuttgart: Ferdinand Enke Verlag.

Lukács, G. (1971[1923]) *History and Class Consciousness*. Cambridge, MA: MIT Press.

Lukes, S. (1967) 'Varieties of Political Philosophy', *Political Studies*, 15: 55–9.

Lukes, S. (1973) *Individualism*. Oxford: Basil Blackwell.

Lukes, S. (1974) 'Relativism Cognitive and Moral', *Supplementary Proceedings of the Aristotelian Society*, June; reprinted in Lukes 1977c.

Lukes, S. (1976) 'Reply to Bradshaw', *Sociology*, 10: 128–32; reprinted in Scott (ed.) 1994.

Lukes, S. (1977a) 'Power and Structure', in Lukes 1977c.

Lukes, S. (1977b) Reply to MacDonald 1976, *British Journal of Political Science*, 7: 418–19.

Lukes, S. (1977c) *Essays in Social Theory*. London: Macmillan.

Lukes, S. (1978) 'Power and Authority', in T. Bottomore and R. Nisbet (eds), *A History of Sociological Analysis*. London: Heinemann, pp. 633–76.

Lukes, S. (1979) 'On the Relativity of Power', in S. C. Brown (ed.) *Philosophical Disputes in the Social Sciences*. Brighton: Harvester, pp. 261–74.

Lukes, S. (1985) *Marxism and Morality*. Oxford: Oxford University Press.

Lukes, S. (ed.) (1986) *Power*. Oxford: Blackwell; New York: New York University Press.

Lukes, S. (1987) 'Perspectives on Authority', in J. R. Pennock and J. W. Chapman (eds), *Authority Revisited, Nomos*, XXIX; reprinted in Raz (ed.) 1990.

Lukes, S. (1996) 'Potere', in *Enciclopedia delle scienze sociali*, Rome: Treccani, 6: 722–45.

Lukes, S. (2002) 'Power and Agency' (review article about Hayward 2000), *British Journal of Sociology*, 53: 491–6.

Lukes, S. (2003) 'Le pouvoir dans l'oeuvre de Coleman', *Revue française de sociologie*, 44: 375–88.

MacDonald, K. I. (1976) 'Is "Power" Essentially Contested?', *British Journal of Political Science*, 6: 380–2.

Mann, M. (1986) *The Sources of Social Power*, vol. 1: *A History of Power from the Beginning to AD 1760*. New York: Cambridge University Press.

Mann, M. (1993) *The Sources of Social Power*, vol. 2: *The Rise of Classes and Nation-states, 1760–1914*. New York: Cambridge University Press.

March, J. (1966) 'The Power of Power', in D. Easton (ed.), *Varieties of Political Theory*, Englewood Cliffs, NJ: Prentice-Hall.

Marcuse, H. (1964) *One-Dimensional Man: Studies in the Ideology of Advanced Industrial Society*. London: Routledge and Kegan Paul.

Martin, R. (1977) *The Sociology of Power*. London: Routledge & Kegan Paul.

References

Marx, K. (1976[1867]) *Capital*, vol. 1, Introduced by E. Mandel, trans. B. Fowkes. Harmondsworth: Penguin; New York: Vintage.

Marx, K. and Engels, F. (1962) *Selected Works*, 2 vols. Moscow: Foreign Languages Publishing House.

Marx, K. and Engels, F. (1965[1845]) *The German Ideology*. London: Lawrence & Wishart.

Mason, A. (1993) *Explaining Political Disagreement*. Cambridge: Cambridge University Press.

McCarthy, T. (1990) 'The Critique of Impure Reason', *Political Theory*, 18: 437–69; reprinted in Wartenberg (ed.) 1992.

McGary, H. (1992) 'Power, Scientific Research and Self-Censorship', in Wartenberg (ed.) 1992.

McGettigan, T. (2002) 'Redefining Reality: A Resolution to the Paradox of Emancipation and the Agency–Structure Dichotomy', *Theory and Science*, 3, 2.

McHoul, A. and Grace, W. (1993) *A Foucault Primer: Discourse, Power and the Subject*. New York: New York University Press.

McLachlan, H. V. (1981) 'Is "Power" an Evaluative Concept?', *British Journal of Sociology*, 32: 392–410; reprinted in Scott (ed.) 1994.

McNay, L. (1992) *Foucault and Feminism: Power, Gender and the Self*. Cambridge: Polity Press; Boston, MA: Northeastern University Press.

Merelman, R. (1968a) 'On the Neo-elitist Critique of Community Power', *American Political Science Review*, 62: 451–60.

Merelman, R. (1968b) Communication to the Editor, *American Political Science Review*, 62: 1269.

Merquior, J. G. (1979) *The Veil and the Mask: Essays on Culture and Ideology*. London: Routledge & Kegan Paul.

Merquior, J. G. (1991) *Foucault*, 2nd edn. London: Fontana.

Miliband, R. (1969) *The State in Capitalist Society*. London: Weidenfeld & Nicolson.

Miliband, R. (1970) 'The Capitalist State: Reply to Nicolas Poulantzas', *New Left Review*, 59: 53–60.

Miliband, R. (1973) 'Poulantzas and the Capitalist State', *New Left Review*, 82: 83–92.

Mill, J. S. (1989[1869]) *On the Subjection of Women*, in J. S. Mill, *On Liberty and Other Writings*, ed. Stefan Collini. Cambridge: Cambridge University Press.

Miller, J. B. (1992) 'Women and Power' in Wartenberg (ed.) 1992.

Mills, C. Wright (1956) *The Power Elite*. New York: Oxford University Press; republished in 2000 with a new Afterword by Alan Wolfe.

Mills, C. Wright (1959) *The Causes of World War Three*. London: Secker & Warburg.

Mitchell, T. (1990) 'Everyday Metaphors of Power', *Theory and Society*, 19: 545–77.

Moore, B. (1967) *Social Origins of Dictatorship and Democracy: Lord and Peasant in the Making of the Modern World*. London: Allen Lane.

Morriss, P. (1972) 'Power in New Haven: A Reassessment of "Who Governs?" ', *British Journal of Political Science*, 2: 457–65.

Morriss, P. (1980) 'The Essentially Uncontestable Concepts of Power' in M. Freeman and D. Robertson (eds), *The Frontiers of Political Theory*. New York: St Martin's Press, pp. 198–232.

Morriss, P. (2002) *Power: A Philosophical Analysis*, 2nd edn. Manchester: Manchester University Press; 1st edn 1987.

Nagel, J. H. (1975) *The Descriptive Analysis of Power*. New Haven, CT: Yale University Press.

Newton, K. (1972) 'Democracy, Community Power and Non-decision making', *Political Studies*, 20: 484–7.

Nietzsche, F. (1956[1887]) *The Genealogy of Morals* in *The Birth of Tragedy and The Genealogy of Morals*, trans. F. Golffing. Garden City, NY: Doubleday.

Nietzsche, F. (1967[1908]) *Ecce Homo*, trans. W. Kaufmann. New York: Vintage.

Nietzsche, F. (1968[1906]) *The Will to Power*, trans. W. Kaufmann and R. J. Hollingdale. New York: Vintage.

Nietzsche, F. (1974[1882,1887]) *The Gay Science*, trans. W. Kaufmann. New York: Vintage.

Nozick, R. (1972) 'Coercion', in P. Laslett and W. G. Runciman (eds), *Philosophy, Politics and Society*, 4th Series. Oxford: Basil Blackwell, pp. 101–35.

Nussbaum, M. C. (2000) *Women and Human Development: The Capabilities Approach*. Cambridge and New York: Cambridge University Press.

Nussbaum, M. C. and Glover, J. (1995) *Women, Culture and Development*. Oxford: Clarendon Press.

Nussbaum, M. and Sen, A. (eds) (1993) *The Quality of Life*. Oxford: Clarendon Press.

Okin, S. M. (1989) *Justice, Gender and the Family*. New York: Basic Books.

Oppenheim, F. E. (1981) *Political Concepts: A Reconstruction*. Chicago, IL: Chicago University Press.

Parsons, T. (1957) 'The Distribution of Power in American Society', *World Politics*, 10: 123–43 (a review article of Mills 1956).

Parsons, T. (1963a) 'On the Concept of Political Power', *Proceedings of the American Philosophical Society*, 107: 232–62; reprinted in Bell *et al.* (ed.) 1969 and Lukes (ed.) 1986.

Parsons, T. (1963b) 'On the Concept of Political Influence', *Public Opinion Quarterly*, 27: 37–62.

Parsons, T. (1967) *Sociological Theory and Modern Society*. New York: Free Press.

Pasquino, P. (1992) 'Political Theory of War and Peace: Foucault and the History of Modern Political Theory', *Economy and Society*, 21: 77–89.

Peck, J. and Tickell, A. (2002) 'Neoliberalizing Space', *Antipode*, 34: 380–403.

Pennock, J. R. and Chapman, J. W. (eds) (1972) *Coercion, Nomos*, 14. New York: Aldine-Atherton.

Pettit, P. (1996) 'Freedom as Antipower', *Ethics*, 106: 576–604.

Pettit, P. (1997) *Republicanism: A Theory of Freedom and Government*. Oxford: Clarendon Press.

Pettit, P. (2001) *A Theory of Freedom: From the Psychology to the Politics of Agency*. Cambridge: Polity Press.

Poggi, G. (2001) *Forms of Power*. Cambridge: Polity Press.

Polsby, N. W. (1968) 'Community: the Study of Community Power', in D. Sills (ed.), *International Encyclopedia of the Social Sciences*. New York: Macmillan and Free Press, 3: 157–63.

Polsby, N. W. (1963) *Community Power and Political Theory*, 2nd edn 1980. New Haven, CT: Yale University Press.

Popitz, H. (1986) *Phänomene der Macht*. Tübingen: J. C. B. Mohr.

Poulantzas, N. (1969) 'The Problem of the Capitalist State', *New Left Review*, 58: 67–78.

Poulantzas, N. (1973) *Political Power and Social Classes*. London: New Left Books, Sheed and Ward.

Poulantzas, N. (1976) 'The Capitalist State: a Reply to Miliband and Laclau', *New Left Review*, 95: 63–83.

References

Przeworski, A. (1980) 'Material Bases of Consent: Economics and Politics in a Hegemonic System', in M. Zeitlin (ed.), *Political Power and Social Theory*, vol. 1, Greenwich, CT: JAI Press, pp. 21–66.

Przeworski, A. (1985) *Capitalism and Social Democracy*. Cambridge: Cambridge University Press; Paris: Editions de la Maison des Sciences de l'Homme.

Przeworski, A. (1998) 'Deliberation and Ideological Domination', in J. Elster (ed.), *Deliberative Democracy*. Cambridge: Cambridge University Press, pp. 140–60.

Rawls, J. (1972) *A Theory of Justice*. Oxford: Clarendon Press.

Raz, J. (1979) *The Authority of Law: Essays on Law and Morality*. Oxford: Clarendon Press.

Raz, J. (ed.) (1990) *Authority*. New York: New York University Press.

Riker, W. H. (1964) 'Some Ambiguities in the Notion of Power', *American Political Science Review*, 58: 341–9; reprinted in Bell et al. (eds) 1969.

Riker, W. H. (1986) *The Art of Political Manipulation*. New Haven, CT: Yale University Press.

Rorty, A. O. (1992) 'Power and Powers: a Dialogue between Buff and Rebuff', in Wartenberg (ed.) 1992.

Rose, N. (1999) *Powers of Freedom: Reframing Political Thought*. Cambridge: Cambridge University Press.

Rosen, M. (1996) *On Voluntary Servitude: False Consciousness and the Theory of Ideology*. Cambridge: Polity Press.

Rothschild, K. W. (ed.) (1971) *Power in Economics: Selected Readings*. Harmondsworth: Penguin Books.

Russell, B. (1938) *Power: A New Social Analysis*. London: Allen & Unwin.

Said, E. (1986) 'Foucault and the Imagination of Power', in Hoy (ed.) 1986.

Sawicki, J. (1991) *Disciplining Foucault: Feminism, Power and the Body*. New York: Routledge.

Schattschneider, E. E. (1960) *The Semi-Sovereign People: A Realist's View of Democracy in America*. New York: Holt, Rhinehart & Winston.

Scheler, M. (1972) *Ressentiment*. New York: Schocken Books.

Schumpeter, J. A. (1962[1950]) *Capitalism, Socialism and Democracy*, 3rd edn. Harper Torchbooks edition: New York: Harper and Row.

Scott, J. (ed.) (1994) *Power: Critical Concepts*. 3 vols. London: Routledge.

Scott, J. (2001) *Power*. Cambridge: Polity Press.

References

Scott, J. C. (1985) *Weapons of the Weak: Everyday Forms of Peasant Resistance*. New Haven, CT: Yale University Press.

Scott, J. C. (1990) *Domination and the Arts of Resistance: Hidden Transcripts*. New Haven, CT: Yale University Press.

Sen, A. (1984) *Resources, Values and Development*. Oxford: Basil Blackwell; Cambridge, MA: Harvard University Press.

Sen, A. (1985) *Commodities and Capabilities*. Amsterdam: North-Holland.

Sen, A. (1992) *Inequality Re-examined*. Oxford: Oxford University Press; Cambridge, MA: Harvard University Press.

Sen, A. (2002) *Rationality and Freedom*. Cambridge, MA: Harvard University Press.

Sennett, R. (2003) *Respect in a World of Inequality*. New York: W. W. Norton.

Shapiro, I. (2003) *The State of Democratic Theory*. Princeton, NJ: Princeton University Press.

Somjee, A. H. (1972) 'Political Dynamics of a Gujarat Village', *Asian Survey*, 12(7): 602–8.

Spinoza, B. de (1958[1677]) *Tractatus Politicus*, in B. de Spinoza, *The Political Works*, ed. and trans. A. G. Wernham. Oxford: Clarendon Press.

Spivak, G. C. (1992) 'More on Power/Knowledge', in Wartenberg (ed.) 1992.

Srinivas, M. N. (1952) *Religion and Society among the Coorgs of South India*. Oxford: Clarendon Press.

Srinivas, M. N. (1962) *Caste in Modern India and Other Essays*. London: Asia Publishing House.

Stone, C. (1980) 'Systemic Power in Community Decision-Making: a Restatement of Stratification Theory', *American Political Science Review*, 74(4): 978–90.

Stoppino, M. (1995) *Potere e teoria politica*. Milan: Giuffré.

Strange, S. (1990) 'Finance, Information and Power', *Review of International Studies*, 16: 259–74.

Strawson, P. F. (1959) *Individuals*. London: Methuen.

Sunstein, C. R. (1997) *Free Markets and Social Justice*. Oxford: Oxford University Press.

Swanton, C. (1985) 'On the "Essential Contestedness" of Political Concepts', *Ethics*, 95: 811–27.

Swidler, A. (1986) 'Culture in Action: Symbols and Strategies', *American Sociological Review*, 51: 273–86.

References

Tambiah, S. J. (1968) 'The Magical Power of Words', *Journal of the Royal Anthropological Institute*, 3: 175–208.

Taylor, C. (1984) 'Foucault on Freedom and Truth', *Political Theory*, 12(2): 152–83; reprinted in Taylor 1985.

Taylor, C. (1985) *Philosophical Papers*, vol. 1: *Human Agency and Language*; vol. 2: *Philosophy and the Human Sciences*. Cambridge: Cambridge University Press.

Taylor, C. (1992) *Multiculturalism and 'The Politics of Recognition': An Essay by Charles Taylor*, ed. with commentary by A. Gutmann et al. Princeton, NJ: Princeton University Press.

Therborn, G. (1980) *The Ideology of Power and the Power of Ideology*. London: Verso.

Thomas, K. (1978) 'Power and Autonomy: Further Comments on the Many Faces of Power', *Sociology*, 12: 332–5.

Tilly, C. (1991) 'Domination, Resistance, Compliance ... Discourse', *Sociological Forum*, 6 (3): 593–602.

Urbinati, N. (2002) *Mill on Democracy: From the Athenian Polis to Representative Government*. Chicago, IL: University of Chicago Press.

Urry, J. and Wakeford, J. (eds) (1973) *Power in Britain: Sociological Readings*. London: Heinemann Educational.

van den Berg, A. (1998) 'Is Sociological Theory Too Grand for Social Mechanisms?' in Hedström and Swedberg (eds) 1998.

Vico, G. (1963[1744]) *La Scienza nuova secondo l'edizione del 1744*. Milan: Rizzoli.

Wacquant, L. (2003) *Body and Soul: Notebooks of an Apprentice Boxer*. New York: Oxford University Press.

Walker, J. L. (1966) 'A Critique of the Elitist Theory of Democracy', *American Political Science Review*, 60: 285–95; reprinted in Scott (ed.) 1994.

Wartenberg, T. E. (1990) *The Forms of Power: From Domination to Transformation*. Philadelphia, PA: Temple University Press.

Wartenberg, T. E. (ed.) (1992) *Rethinking Power*. Albany, NY: State University of New York Press.

Weber, M. (1978[1910–14]) *Economy and Society*, ed. G. Roth and C. Wittich. Berkeley, CA: California University Press.

Wertheimer, A. (1987) *Coercion*. Princeton, NJ: Princeton University Press.

West, D. (1987) 'Power and Formation: New Foundations for a Radical Concept of Power', *Inquiry*, 30: 137–54.

References

White, D. M. (1971) 'Power and Intention', *American Political Science Review*, 65 (3): 749–59.

White, D. M. (1972) 'The Problem of Power', *British Journal of Political Science*, 2 (4): 479–90.

White, M, (1978) *Power Politics*, ed. H. Bull and C. Holbraad. Leicester: Leicester University Press and Royal Institute of International Affairs.

Williams, G. A. (1960) 'The Concept of "Egemonia" in the Thought of Antonio Gramsci: Some Notes on Interpretation', *Journal of the History of Ideas*, 21(4): 586–99.

Willis, P. (1977) *Learning to Labour*. Westmead: Saxon House.

Wolf, E. R. (1999) *Envisioning Power: Ideologies of Dominance and Crisis*. Berkeley, CA: University of California Press.

Wolf, E. R. (2001) *Pathways of Power: Building an Anthropology of the New World: Essays by Eric R. Wolf with Sydal Silverman*. Berkeley, CA: University of California Press.

Wolfe, A. (2000) New Afterword to Mills 1956. New York: Oxford University Press.

Wolfinger, R. E. (1971a) 'Nondecisions and the Study of Local Politics', *American Political Science Review*, 65: 1063–80.

Wolfinger, R. E. (1971b) 'Rejoinder to Frey's "Comment"', *American Political Science Review*, 65: 1102–4.

Wollstonecraft, M. (1988[1792]) *A Vindication of the Rights of Women, with Strictures on Political and Moral Subjects*, ed. Carol H. Poston, Second Norton Critical Edition. New York: W. W. Norton.

Wrong, D. (1979) *Power: Its Forms, Bases and Uses*. Oxford: Basil Blackwell.

Young I. M. (1988) 'Five Faces of Oppression', *The Philosophical Forum*, 19: 270–90; reprinted in Wartenberg (ed.) 1992.

Young, I. M. (1990) *Justice and the Politics of Difference*. Princeton, NJ: Princeton University Press.

Young, R. A. (1978) 'Steven Lukes's Radical View of Power', *Canadian Journal of Political Science*, 1: 639–49.

INDEX

Note: Figures and charts are indicated by bold, italicized type.

Index

'Critique of the Ruling Elite
Model, A', 4

Dahl, Robert
  critique of, 60–1
  and pluralism (one-dimensional
    power), 4–5, 15–19, 23, 27,
    38–9, 152 n.4
decision-making
  control of, 2–3, 6, 28, 40, 45
  limitations of, 6, 20–5, 47
  and pluralism, 5, 17–18, 39
democracy, 6, 17
discipline *see* Foucault
Discipline and Punish, 90, 92
Distinction, 142
Dominant Ideology Thesis, The, 130
domination
  as conceptualized by Bourdieu,
    140, 142
  as conceptualized by Foucault, 90,
    92
  explanations of, 10–11
  and false consciousness, 144–6
  and power, 84–6, 109–14,
    118–20, 123–4, 150
  and powerlessness, 67–8
Domination and the Arts of Resistance,
    124
Donzelot, Jacques, 101–2
dual consciousness, 49–52, 120,
    144–5
DuBois, W. E. B., 120

education, 104–6
'egemonia' *see* hegemony
Elster, Jon, 13, 134–6, 156 n.2, 162
    n.17
Engels, Fredrich, 152 n.1
expert knowledge *see* Foucault

false consciousness, 19, 123, 126,
    144–6, 149–50
  see also hegemony
families, 101–2

Fanon, Frantz, 120
fields *see* Bourdieu
first-dimension (of power), **29**, 38–9,
    58
Flyvbjerg, Bent, 102–3
force, 21–2, 32–4, **36**, 87
Foucault, Michel
  and discipline, 90, 92–3, 99, 102,
    104–6, 158 n.22
  and domination, 12, 60–1, 87, 90,
    92, 94, 97–8
  and identity, 89, 96–7, 121, 123
  and knowledge, 88, 101, 103
  and normalization, 91, 101–2
  and power, 89–107, 123, 157 n.18
  and resistance, 95, 158 nn.26 and
    n.27
Frankfurt School, 8
Fraser, Nancy, 90
freedom, 114–18
functional explanation, 135–6, 162
    n.17
Frey, Frederick, 15, 59

Garland, David, 89, 92, 158 n.23
Gaventa, John, 130–1
Giddens, Anthony, 33
governmentality, 91, 96
Gramsci, Antonio, 7–8, 49–50,
    144–5, 152 n.1
grievances *see* preferences

habitus *see* Bourdieu
Hayward, Clarissa, 103–6, 159 n.33
hegemony
  and consent, 7–10
  and false consciousness, 123,
    125–6, 128–31
  and real interests, 144–5, 152 n.1
hidden transcript *see* Scott
History of Sexuality, 91, 94
Hobbes, Thomas, 62, 66
human body
  and micro-physics of power, 88–93

Index

Index